The Beaver Papers

The Story of the Lost Season

30th Anniversary Edition

Will Jacobs & Gerard Jones

 Atomic Drop Press

Rededicated to
Theron "Chip" Kabrich and Jim Zook
because they laughed so hard
for so long.

Foreword to the New Edition

Although my area of expertise is literature, not sitcoms, I can't think of a more felicitous blending of the two than the book you now hold in your hands (or peer at on your iPhone).

I'll admit that I was never much of a *Leave It to Beaver* fan when I was growing up. The show was cancelled in 1963, nearly fifteen years before I was born. I caught it in rerun a few times, but I was never able to get what the fuss was all about. Fortunately for our literary heritage, however, a great many people did get it, foremost among them the world's literati of half a century ago. The book's original introduction delves into this seminal moment in our history; suffice it to say here that when news of *Beaver's* cancellation was announced, a global effort was launched in the hopes of reversing the decision, and writers and filmmakers from Yukio Mishima to Ingmar Bergman submitted scripts in an effort to inject new blood into the failing show.

The Beaver Papers was first published in 1983. I was only five at the time, and not destined to discover it until my freshman year in junior college. One sparkling autumn day in 1997 I stopped at a garage sale in Pomona and spotted a dog-eared copy of the book sticking out of a box of bathroom scales. At first glance I nearly dismissed it. I recognized Jerry Mathers on the cover and assumed the book was about the TV show that I had seen but a handful of times and held in very low regard. Not even the vaguely pornographic title stirred my interest. But then my eyes moved to the left hand column and my heart nearly stopped!

Under the title and subtitle, the text proclaimed that within these pages were to be found script treatments by the likes of Jack Kerouac, John Steinbeck, Samuel Beckett, and Tennessee Williams! Heart racing, I flipped to the table of contents and saw that the list of literary luminaries went on and on. A heartbeat later my dime was in the palm of the sweaty old coot running the sale, and I was racing home to devour my newfound treasure.

Maybe you're a voracious reader like me, and you number among the saddest moments in your life those occasions when you've finished off a writer's catalogue and realize that there's nothing new left to read by him. Even at a mere nineteen years of age I had already devoured all of Faulkner, Hemingway, Steinbeck, and Kerouac. Imagine my delight when, having thought that I'd never again read anything new by these writers, I was suddenly treated to *The Beaver and the Fury, A Clean Well-Lighted Beaver, The Beaver of Wrath,* and *Dharma Beaver!* Granted, the book only contains summaries of the scripts, but Jacobs and Jones had done such a sterling job of preserving each writer's style that I hardly noticed the difference.

This amazing ability to capture the essence of a writer's lifeblood is again very much in evidence in the two new scripts included in this book as a sneak preview to the forthcoming *The Beaver Papers 2*. If Jacobs and Jones's adaptations of *Midnight Beaver* by James Leo Herlihy and *The Electric Kool-Aid Kleaver Picnic* by Tom Wolfe are any indication of what's in store, then the sequel—as is so rarely the case—may actually eclipse the original.

So enthralled did I become with the original version of the book that I found myself turning on my television every day at precisely ten a.m. to catch reruns of the show, even if it meant cutting the occasional class. Although it would be foolish to claim that the six seasons that actually aired could ever be a match for the glory promised by the "lost" seventh season, I began to see what so many others had seen before me. I constantly found myself catching echoes of the "fabled" season in these old episodes. When Lumpy, amorphous, slack-jawed and vacant-eyed, showed up to visit Wally, I could visualize precisely what Steinbeck had in mind when he cast him as the rabbit-hungry simpleton. When June is forever shown lining shelves and making lemonade, I could see why Vonnegut would posit the need for a "Humanizer" to make the Cleavers "more like other people." And every time the Cleavers sat down to dinner and Beaver and Wally dominated the table talk with their cute, innocuous comments, I saw why Hemingway chose the word *"nada"* to capture the essential quality of life in Mayfield.

If I may be allowed to interject a personal note, I was stunned and delighted to find mentioned within the pages of *The Beaver Papers* an essay entitled "Beaver: Child, Rodent, or Organ," contributed by none other than my grandfather, the late Lionel Endenberry, LittD. This came as a complete surprise to me. In all the golden years of my childhood, sitting on the old man's knee and listening to him expound on mimesis and parataxis, he never once mentioned a beaver of any sort. And yet there he was and always shall be. As another scholar discussed in the book, Carl Jung, once remarked, the synchronicities abound!

In closing, I wish to offer my heartfelt thanks to Atomic Drop Press for honoring me with the opportunity to write this introduction. I feel a great affinity with Will Jacobs and Gerard Jones. Like them, and like the great Poggio Bracciolini before them who dug up so many of the literary treasures of antiquity in the ruins of medieval Europe, I too had the good fortune to unearth a treasure trove of forgotten literature, as *The Max Kleinman Reader* (selected by Atom Drop Press to launch their publishing line) clearly attests. But whereas I only rescued one writer—albeit a titan among his peers—Jacobs and Jones have salvaged dozens of lost literary masterworks.

At least that's what Jacobs and Jones asked me to say. And since I don't know how long it will be until someone else asks me to write a foreword to a book, I had no intention of refusing. Make of it what you will.

Lionel Endenberry
Editor of *The Max Kleinman Reader*

Introduction to the New Edition

A lot has happened in thirty years, but through it all we have always hoped for a chance to republish *The Beaver Papers*. Not only was it our first published book, not only was it the one we invested the most time in—with countless hours spent poring through dusty boxes of forgotten scripts and correspondence—but, as we explain below, it was also the project we never truly got to finish.

Rereading our work from thirty years ago, we found plenty of passages that we would word differently now. We were tempted to rewrite them, we'll admit, but we've always been uneasy about writers who weren't willing to stand by their youthful idiosyncrasies. As William Saroyan, himself a proud contributor to *The Beaver Papers,* said in his introduction to the second edition of *The Man on the Flying Trapeze,* "There are many things I can do as a writer now that I couldn't then, but also things I did then that I could never do now." (Actually, we couldn't find our copy of the book at press time, so that isn't an exact quote. But it was a lot like that.) Therefore, we have chosen to reproduce the original edition except to correct typos and clear errors of fact. This time we've also been able to ascribe authorship to several scripts that we had to run anonymously before due to then-unresolved legal issues with the authors.

It has always been our hope to make available all the material generated by the world's great writers and intellectuals in their heroic effort to save *Leave It to Beaver,* the dozens of full scripts, the many scholarly tomes, reproductions of the stunning works of art. Now Atomic Drop Press has given us the opportunity to bring to the world much of what we had to leave out of the original. A great many unpublished scripts and further accounts of the events surrounding them will be appearing, at long last, in *The Beaver Papers 2.* Look for it in 2014.

But let's not get ahead of ourselves. We are thrilled to have the chance, after three decades, to welcome back into publication the book that started it all: *The Beaver Papers.*

Will Jacobs and Gerard Jones
September 2013

The Beaver Papers

Castor vincit omnia.

Luticrus

Contents

Notes on behind-the-scenes events appear between the scripts

Prologue

On May 3, 1963, the news filtered down from ABC to Bob
Mosher and Joe Connelly that *Leave It to Beaver* would
probably be canceled. Just a month before, network
executives had told Mosher and Connelly, producers and
head writers of the show, that if new blood could be put
into *Beaver,* the series might be saved. But after weeks of
frustrating meetings with regular writers Dick Conway and
Roland MacLane and multi-talented director-star Hugh
Beaumont, it was conceded that no new ideas could be
contrived.

Mosher suggested an episode in which brother Wally
gets drunk on near-beer, but Connelly vetoed it as being too
outlandish. Connelly suggested an episode in which June
appeared in a pair of slacks, but Beaumont considered it
lewd. Beaumont suggested an episode in which Beaver
actually metamorphosed into a rodent, but Mosher and
Connelly denounced it as derivative.

MacLane and Conway completed a script in which Beaver
gets a flat tire on his bike and conceals it from his parents,
but network executives, although impressed with its daring,
decided that it didn't quite fit their standards for new blood.

By May 5 the staff had cleared their desks and prepared
to go to pasture when, with the afternoon mail delivery, the
first submission arrived.

Clearly the news of the impending cancellation had leaked out quickly, evidently reaching as far as Lowell, Massachusetts, for Jack Kerouac was the first to rise in support of Beaver. His script, *Dharma Beaver,* was the first drop in a deluge of literary brilliance to flood the network offices. From Montmartre and Tokyo they flowed in; from North Beach and Greenwich Village; from Majorca and Fresno; and from as far away as Moscow and Nigeria. The cry rang like a trumpet blast through the artistic community of the globe: "The Beaver is endangered! Save the Beaver!" Even the petition to free Jean Genet from prison did not inspire such solidarity among the literati of the world. Before the summer was through, mankind would witness a flowering of the arts such as it had not seen since the Italian Renaissance.

Now, after years of diligent research into old studio files, we have pieced together the story of the "Lost Season." We present here the events of that summer, along with summaries of the twenty-five unproduced scripts that were slated for the 1963-1964 season of *Leave It to Beaver.*

We have endeavored to preserve the writing style and dialogue of the scripts wherever possible. The fruits of the "Lost Season" have been harvested at last.

May 5, 1963

Jack Kerouac, leading voice of the Beat Generation, often wrote about the search for America. Here, on the heels of his *Big Sur,* he brings to light the search theme that was always latent in *Leave It to Beaver.*

Dharma Beaver

Jack Kerouac

Eddie steals a bike and passes Mary Ellen Rogers's house on the way to Wally's. Mary Ellen, on the porch with her friend Elma, nudges her and says, "There goes Eddie Haskell. I wonder where he's going to?" Elma looks mystified and says, "I wonder where he's coming from?"

At Wally's, Eddie says, "Hey, Sam, what state are we in?" Wally, at his desk in his bedroom, typing on a huge roll of paper, says, "Aw, go on, Eddie, I don't have time to think about things like that. I'm writing a novel." Eddie says, "Oh, yeah? Do you have time to notice that?" He points to the bike out the window. "Gee, where'd you get the new wheels?" asks Wally. Beaver, reading *A Coney Island of the Mind,* says, "Aw, he probably swiped it." Eddie says, "Shut up, squirt. You don't know the meaning of Beat."

Beaver asks, "Hey, Wally, what direction is San Francisco from here?" Wally looks mystified: "Gee, I dunno, Beav. In geography class they told us it was on the West Coast, but..." Eddie says, "Come on, Gertrude, don't be such a square. Why do you think I swiped the wheels? These old-timers don't know any more about where we are than we do. We've got to find out for ourselves." "Gosh, I don't know, Eddie," says Wally. But Eddie insists and Wally finally agrees. Eddie says, "All we've got to do is make tracks until we get to some city we've heard of. Then we'll know what state we're in."

On the way out of Mayfield they pass the Rutherfords', where Lumpy is sitting in a lotus position on the front lawn. When the boys ask him what he's doing, Lumpy responds, "I'm getting ready for my trip to Japan." Wally says, "Gee, you mean your dad's letting you go? What are you gonna do there?" Lumpy says, "I'm gonna be a Buddhist monk and write poetry." "A Buddhist monk, Sam?" says Eddie. "Those old Chinamen won't let you eat!" Lumpy says, "Really? Gosh, Daddy didn't tell me that." Wally asks, "By the way, Lumpy, what direction is Japan from here?"

They pass a road sign reading BELL PORT, 5 MILES. Wally says, "Gee, Eddie, it's like we're in search of America." Eddie says, "To hell with that, Sam. I just want to know where in America we are."

They arrive in Bell Port, buy a bottle of whiskey, drink themselves blind, and recite Ginsberg's *Howl* in chorus. They accost strangers and ask where they are. Unanimously, the strangers answer, "In Bell Port." They ask, "But where's Bell Port?" The strangers look at them, mystified, and walk away.

They awake among empty bottles in a sleazy hotel. Suddenly Ward enters to take them home. At home, in the den, Ward says, "When I was your age, Wally, I went looking for America too. But then I realized that this was America, right here in Mayfield." Wally says, "Sure, Dad. But what part of America?" Ward looks mystified.

Tag: Beaver bursts into the boys' bedroom waving an envelope. "Hey, Wally! Hey, Wally! Look, you got a letter from Viking Press." Wally opens the envelope and says, "Holy Cow, Beav. They're publishing my novel." Beaver teases him good-naturedly in his screeching falsetto: "Bookworm! Bookworm!" Wally good-naturedly hits him with a pillow.

May 5–10, 1963

Mosher and Connelly were frankly perplexed by this submission. Although horrified at Kerouac's new interpretation of Eddie and Wally's morality, they were nonetheless flattered that such a literary giant would contribute to their show. Having nothing to lose, they presented the script to ABC executives. While they did not recognize Kerouac's name, the executives did seem tentatively interested in this new direction.

Mosher and Connelly then showed the script to the cast. Hugh Beaumont, who brought Ward Cleaver to life on the show, commented, "I like the idea of Wally wanting to be a writer. I did a little writing myself when I was a young man." Stanley Fafara, who played Beaver's little friend Whitey Whitney, praised the references to Ferlinghetti and Ginsberg, whose works he greatly admired.

Mosher and Connelly telegraphed Kerouac, asking if he would care to work with Roland MacLane and Dick Conway on future episodes should ABC reverse its decision to cancel the show. While they waited for a response, the second submission arrived.

The Gomalco Productions offices were rocked by the arrival in the mail of *The Beaver of Wrath* by Nobel Prize winner John Steinbeck. In this script, the aging Steinbeck seeks out the essential kinship between the migrants of the depression, whom he eulogized, and the Cleaver family, who epitomize for him the fulfillment of the promise of the Joads.

The Beaver of Wrath

John Steinbeck

The gray soil of Metzger's Field turns to white and the red tanbark of the schoolyard is burned a pale pink by the sun. The people of Mayfield, the people of the land from Camelback Cutoff down to Bell Port, watch Miller's Pond dry into its own mud.

Beaver walks down the road toward home, just released from Saturday school detention for punching Larry Mondello in the stomach. He finds the people of Mayfield streaming out of town in their station wagons. Eddie Haskell wanders by, philosophizing humbly. Beaver says, "Creep! Creep! Creep!" Eddie shakes his head. "Nope, I used to be a creep. But I asked myself, What is it a man can be a creep about? and I knew it was only hisself. I heard you punched a squirt." Beaver says, "Yeah, and I'd do it again if I had to."

They find Ward, in golf sweater, tie, and overalls, squatting in the front yard, drawing patterns in the dust with his newspaper. Wally squats beside him, saying, "Gee, Pa, it's Satiddy afternoon and thar ain't no water in the pond. The fambly ain't got a chancet of a good picnic now." June says, "I seen in the picture books oncet how they's water up to Friend's Lake. I'd like to get me one o' them little picnic tables with trees all around." She spies Beaver and says,

"Praise Gawd for vittory! Now I got my whole Cleaver fambly about me agin! And if it ain't the old creep!"

Eddie says, "Good afternoon, Mrs. Cleaver, but I ain't a creep no more. No man's got business bein' more of a creep than any other." June loads the station wagon with pork bones and baloney sandwiches. Gilbert, Richard, Whitey, Larry, and Violet Rutherford pile on the luggage rack. Wally leads Lumpy to join them. Lumpy says, "Gosh, will there be rabbits where we're going, Wally?" "Sure, Lump, you'll have lots of rabbits." "Oh, boy, Wally, and can I eat the rabbits, Wally, huh?"

On the way out of town they meet Gus Chong, the old Chinese fireman and crooked merchant. Wally buys Ward a dog and Beaver beats Wally to a pulp. They find work selling frogs at demeaning wages. In moral outrage, Eddie becomes a creep again and is beaten up by Richard and Gilbert. Beaver is bruised and knows he must go.

June struggles to keep her family together, but Beaver says, "Don't think about me bein' gone, Ma. Wherever there's kids in trouble, I'll be there. Wherever there's a creep givin' the business to a squirt, Ma, I'll be there." June dries her tears on the dusty sleeve of her old gingham dress.

Tag: At night, Wally is doing his 'lectronics homework at his desk. Beaver is packing peaches into a crate. He says, "Hey, Wally, are there any brothers in the Bible with the initials W and B?" Wally says, "Gosh, Beav, I don't know. I ain't no preacher. I'm just a man o' the land." They collapse exhausted into bed and turn out the meager light, but the room goes on glowing warmly.

May 11–14, 1963

Was it just coincidence? Had Kerouac and Steinbeck arrived at their determination independently, or had a call gone out that the sword of Damocles hung over Beaver Cleaver's head? Mosher and Connelly were overjoyed. If the network executives had been impressed by Kerouac, surely the Steinbeck script might dissuade them from their plans of cancellation.

But they were wrong. Although the executives remembered having to read Steinbeck in high school, they didn't "see the commercial potential in a writer for boys."

The cast remained hopeful. Jerry Mathers, as the Beaver, began practicing an Oklahoma accent, t-ing his "onces." Barbara Billingsley, better known as June Cleaver, remarked, "I've always wanted to play a strong woman."

Connelly remained cautious, however. "Me and Bob, we were happy to get the scripts. But the show was still officially canceled, and it was just downright silly to expect anything more to come in. Hoo boy, were we off the mark."

Over a few days, no fewer than seven scripts by world-famous authors arrived at the awestruck offices of Gomalco: Erskine Caldwell's *God's Little Beaver*, Orson Welles's *Citizen Cleaver*, James Leo Herlihy's *Midnight Beaver*, Henry Miller's *Tropic of Beaver*, Philip Roth's *Beaver's Complaint*, Truman Capote's *Breakfast at Beaver's*, and William Saroyan's *The Human Beaver*.

Fearing that too many choices would tax the executives' attention spans, Mosher and Connelly informed them of the flood of submissions but chose to pitch only one—that of America's favorite sentimental Armenian—for the prospective seventh season.

The Human Beaver

William Saroyan

Beaver wakes up to find Wally gone. He dresses and goes downstairs to ask June, "Hey, Mom, did Wally go off to war?" June looks perplexed and calls Ward at the office, asking, "Ward, is there a war on?" Ward: "Why do you ask, dear?" June: "Because Wally isn't home this morning." Ward chuckles and says, "Wally's working for Western Union now, dear." At that moment we see Wally whiz by on his bicycle. June looks after him with heartwarming motherly concern. Beaver opens the refrigerator and hands his mother an egg, by which he means what no man can guess and no beaver can articulate to tell. As he leaves, she looks after him with boundless joy.

Beaver finds Richard sitting in Metzger's Field staring at the ground. Beaver: "Whatcha doin', Richard?" Richard: "Aw, I dunno, Beav. I was just watchin' a gopher and thinkin' how beautiful life is." Just then Wally whizzes by on his bicycle.

Walking toward Miller's Pond, they find Gilbert passed out on a bench. They revive him and buy him a cup of coffee. Beaver: "Hey, what's wrong, Gilbert?" Gilbert lights a cigarette and says, "I haven't eaten for two weeks because I'm writing a book." Richard: "Gee, Gil, doesn't your mom feed you?" Gilbert: "Sure she does, but if I ate everything she feeds me it wouldn't be romantic." Beaver: "Every man is a good dream in a nightmare of a world." They turn to see if Wally is whizzing by on his bicycle. Instead they see an old black man waving at them from the back of a train. They wave back and run jubilantly home to tell their mothers.

As June prepares a dinner of beans and rice, Beaver finds Ward in the den, smoking cigarettes and drinking coffee. Beaver: "Dad, can I ask you a question?" Ward: "Why, of course, Beaver." Beaver: "What country did our family come from?" Ward: "Why, we're from the old country, Beaver." Beaver says, "Gee, thanks, Dad," and gives him an egg. They wait for Wally to come home to dinner, but he does not. June: "Maybe Wally isn't coming home after all." The doorbell rings. June finds Eddie Haskell standing outside, supporting himself on a cane. With tears in her eyes, she brings him to the table.

Tag: Wally tells Beaver in the bedroom: "Love is riding a bike. And if you ride my bike, that is your love for me." Beaver: "Would you let a Turk ride your bike?" Wally throws a pillow at him. Beaver throws an egg at Wally.

May 15–21, 1963

In the face of this deluge of submissions, the ABC
executives appeared to be wavering in their determination
to cancel the series. They were even more impressed
when Hugh Beaumont circulated a memorandum
informing them that these authors were published and well
known outside of television and were, incidentally, held in
high esteem by the literary community. They had heard of
Mr. Welles, having once approached him to host a game
show for ABC.

The cast was ecstatic. Ken Osmond looked forward to
playing a lame, tubercular Eddie Haskell in *Midnight
Beaver*. Sue Randall, the young teacher Miss Landers in the
series, was titillated by the prospect of the violent seduction
scene in *God's Little Beaver*. Beaumont hoped that *Tropic
of Beaver* would be filmed on location in Paris, but after
being told that this was impossible, he reflected, "Being
around the boys so long, I get carried away by youthful zeal
myself sometimes."

Mosher recalled, "Me and Joe, we always wanted to try
our hand at some Wellesian direction. Shoot, but I sure like
those fancy camera angles." All in all, the mood was one of
jubilation.

The arrival of scripts from overseas was doubly
surprising. "First of all, we were thrilled that *Beaver* could
be so meaningful to people in other lands," remarked

18

cowriter Roland MacLane. "And second, we didn't even know the show was being broadcast over there." Tortured Swedish cinematic genius Ingmar Bergman's script was the first.

Cries and Beavers

Ingmar Bergman

OPENING SCENE. JUNE is seen stirring a pot against a blank wall. A clock ticks ominously in the background. The camera closes in on the contents of the pot. It is boiling tomato soup. We see JUNE'S face in an expressionless close-up. She plunges her hand into the boiling soup and screams.

LIVING ROOM. WARD and JUNE sit on the couch. WARD is reading the newspaper. JUNE is knitting. WARD looks over the top of the newspaper and smiles at her. JUNE smiles back. When WARD looks away, JUNE plunges a knitting needle into her breast and screams.

IN AN UNSPECIFIED ROOM. JUNE sits at the window staring at the drizzle outside. We hear her narration: *Mother always said I should have been a nun. How often have I wished that I were Swedish? How pretty Christ's blood would have looked on snow. Wally's grown so big these days, so big. I didn't want to eat that haddock last night. If I hadn't, Ward would have looked at me with his eyes like wounds.*

KITCHEN. Soundlessly, BEAVER and WALLY run through, tracking mud. Without expression, JUNE sweeps up after them. She pulls a single bristle from the broom, plunges it into her eye, and screams.

THE FRONT YARD. WALLY is mowing the lawn in the rain. JUNE brings lemonade to him on a tray. She eyes his body covertly. As he wheels the lawn mower toward her she throws herself under it and screams.

THE BOYS' BEDROOM. WALLY sits at his desk doing his homework, JUNE is washing BEAVER'S feet. She hums a somber Bach partita. We hear her narration: *Mother always said I should have been a whore. How pretty Beaver's blood would have looked on my hands. How often have I wished that I had breast cancer? Wally's grown so big these days, so big.* She swabs BEAVER'S ankles with her hair.

Tag: JUNE puts a toaster in a pillowcase and forces BEAVER to hit her on the head with it. She screams.

May 21–26, 1963

Tony Dow, who played Wally, remembered, "Jerry and me used to kid Barbara on the set all the time about how she loved Bergman movies and how Bibi Andersson's influence always used to show through in her portrayal of Mom. We were really happy that she could fulfill her lifelong ambition of acting for Bergman." In the only dissenting opinion, little white-haired Stanley Fafara noted, "Although I am a great aficionado of Mr. Bergman's work, I question whether his obsessive use of bleak symbolism is compatible with the indigenously American Mayfield milieu. Of course, his work is well at home in the northern European cultural context, along with that of Hamsun, Strindberg, and Lagerkvist."

The tension at Gomalco was allayed by the arrival of four more scripts. *Go Tell It to the Beaver* by James Baldwin, *Who's Afraid of Beaver Cleaver?* by Edward Albee, and *Our Beaver of the Flowers* by Jean Genet were all contenders, but for their seventh season Mosher and Connelly chose the submission from depraved Japanese archer and novelist Yukio Mishima. As a result of this script, American filmmakers later turned to Mishima's work to film *The Sailor Who Fell from Grace with the Sea.*

The Sound of Beaver
Yukio Mishima

Wally, with hairless body, dressed only in a jockstrap, is lifting weights in the boys' bedroom. Beaver shoots rubber-tipped arrows at him, which bounce harmlessly off his torso. Beaver grows bored and says, "Me and Richard and Gilbert are gonna go kill a cat." As the boys walk through Metzger's Field looking for a cat, they come upon Whitey Whitney. Taking him behind a blossoming cherry tree, they pull down his pants. Beaver and Gilbert pin him down while Richard approaches from the rear. Whitey squeals horribly.

Later, alone, Beaver contemplates the waves on Miller's Pond in the setting sun. Suddenly realizing that he is late for dinner, he runs home in exquisite fear. But on the way, he stops to kill a cat.

Ward is annoyed with him for being late. Beaver takes pleasure in his revilement. But after a brief fatherly chat in the den, Ward forgives him. Beaver regards him with icy disdain.

That night, Ward creeps out of bed and goes to the den. Sitting on his desk he strips to the waist, oils his body, rouges his left nipple, and awaits the assassin's blade. But Beaver does not appear all night.

The next day, in the office, Fred Rutherford knows that Ward has lost face. Smugly, Fred reports, "My boy

Clarence would have disemboweled me gladly if I'd disgraced myself in his eyes. But brace up, Ward old man. They don't call you Ward Self-Cleaver for nothing." Fred laughs uproariously. Ward fixes a smile on his face, but in his heart he contemplates the misery that he has wrought so joyously for himself. That evening, Ward once again oils his body. He brings his sword out from behind his insurance portfolios. As he makes the first penetration into his abdomen, June interrupts him: "We're having pot roast tonight, dear." Ward decides to postpone his suicide, perhaps indefinitely. In the background, we hear a cat squeal horribly.

Tag: Beaver is contemplating Wally's proudly erect member. He laughs suddenly and shoots it with a rubber-tipped arrow. Wally hits him with a pillow.

May 26–June 1, 1963

The cast, although flattered by this new celebrity attention, had reservations about the homosexual themes inherent in Mishima's and Genet's scripts. Ken Osmond said, "I've gotten used to playing a bad guy, but being a French convict who gets sodomized all the time would be going too far." Hugh Beaumont cautioned, "I don't know if word's gotten out that we're all camping on the lot, but I don't want any ugly rumors starting just because the men outnumber the women."

Indeed, the dedicated Gomalcoites had chosen en masse to set up cots and Coleman lanterns throughout the ersatz Mayfield. Barbara Billingsley and Doris "Mrs. Rayburn" Packer were put in charge of the chow detail, while the men worked to make the living arrangements more homey. Sue Randall was assigned to handle Tuesday night entertainment, and everyone agreed she did a marvelous job.

The next battle cry to resound in Beaver's defense sprang from the throats of the world's academics. Unable to make any contribution of their own, critics and scholars adapted the styles of great deceased authors to the *Leave It to Beaver* mythos.

The first to be received was Professor Edward Wasiolek's reconstruction of the manner of Feodor Dostoevsky.

The Brothers Cleaver

by Edward Wasiolek in the manner of
Feodor Dostoevsky

Wally is trying to do his homework but Eddie is annoying him. Beaver walks in and says, "Hey, Wally. Do you think it's okay to kill an old lady?" Wally: "Gosh, I don't know, Beav. We haven't gotten that far in civics class." Eddie turns to Beaver and makes the sign of the cross over him. Wally says, "Hey, lay off him, Eddie." Eddie: "Listen, Sam. I gotta do that kind of junk if I want to be a saint." Beaver: "A creep like you is gonna be a saint?" Eddie: "Hey, those saints got it easy. They get obsessed, have visions, contract brain fever, and then they just sit back and wait for the chicks to roll in." Wally and Beaver exchange a dubious glance. Eddie says, "And besides, Gertrude, they even get canonized." Wally looks up, impressed. "Yeah, there's that."

Outside the classroom at school, Lumpy says to Wally, "You know, that Eddie Haskell's got it made. He's got his own tenement hovel, his own body lice, and he's even coming down with consumption. He told me that if I become a saint I could get Mary Ellen Rogers, but my daddy won't let me."

Just then Eddie appears, gaunt, hollow-eyed, and grinning broadly. He says, "Good morning, children. How are things in nursery school?" Wally: "Where were you,

Eddie? You missed a great lecture on moral relativism in philosophy class." Eddie: "Haven't you heard, Sam? Relativism is for squares. All the chicks want a spiritual absolutist. Every night they nearly break my door down to tell me about their latest theological crises. C'mon up and check it out sometime." Just then the bell rings and Wally says, "C'mon, Lump. We're gonna miss our seminar on epilepsy." Lumpy follows reluctantly.

That night at dinner Wally expresses his concern for Eddie: "The visions that dominate Eddie's life corrupt his intellectual purity." Ward passes out drunk. Beaver coughs rackingly. June wraps her shawl around her bony shoulders. Wally storms off in disgust.

Later, when Ward comes to, Beaver says, "Hey, Dad. When I go to high school can I be an ascetic visionary too?" Ward burps and says, "Well, Feodore, sit down and let me tell you a story. There was once a grand inquisitor—" Beaver interrupts. "Dad, is this going to be one of those stories where the grand inquisitor turns out to be you?" Ward beats him senseless with the blunt end of a meat cleaver.

Wally and Lumpy approach Eddie's hovel. Lumpy, delirious with brain fever, continuously mumbles, "Mary Ellen Rogers." They find Eddie delirious with brain fever mumbling, "I didn't kill the old lady. I didn't. I didn't." Wally helps him off his bed of thorns, convinces him that his parents miss him, and reminds him that his beloved cousin Sonya is coming to visit from the country at Easter. Eddie says, "Gee, do you think they'll take me back when they find out how pestilent I am?" Wally says, "Sure, Eddie. They'll put you up in a nice sanatorium."

Tag: Wally and Beaver are coughing rackingly in the bedroom. Their little bodies shiver in the malodorous draft. They clutch their threadbare blankets to their tiny shoulders. When they blow out the flame of their kerosene lamp, the room still glows with an ethereal aura.

June 2–18, 1963

Intellectuals beyond literature were also turning their eyes to Beaver. Most notable among them were Dr. Carl Rogers, who contributed *On Becoming a Beaver,* and Jerry Farber, the author of *Beaver as Nigger.*

Meanwhile, Mosher and Connelly, the Castor and Pollux of Gomalco, had turned all the scripts received so far over to ABC executives. The executives confessed ignorance of all the contributors except Bergman, about whom they were ambivalent. Although they praised her performance in *Casablanca,* they were leery of linking the name of an unmarried mother with *Leave It to Beaver.* Beaumont set them straight about Ingrid and Ingmar.

Due to an impending golf tournament, the executives postponed their cancellation decision.

Developments accelerated week after week. Artists in all fields clamored to make their own contribution to the *Beaver* world view. Frank Lloyd Wright sent in blueprints for his Prairie Cleaver, a modernistic design for the family dwelling, taking into its form the geographic contours of the Mayfield set. Since there were no such geographic contours, this made it a novel edifice indeed. Jazzman Charles Mingus mailed a tape of his polyphonic rendition of the *Beaver* theme song to Gomalco.

In the tumultuous excitement around the Gomalco offices, Mosher and Connelly began to feel creatively frustrated. Like Sisyphus, they had pushed sterile scripts for

29

years up the mountain of literary excellence only to see them slide down again into the mire of hackdom. Connelly remarked, "Me and Bob, we were feeling left out. But after the Russian fellow sent in his Dostoevsky story, we figured, criminy, we could write like dead authors too." So began the phoenix-like rebirth of the talents of Connelly and Mosher.

Feeling that mystery writers had overlooked *Leave It to Beaver* as a source of material, they chose to resurrect the style of Raymond Chandler.

Farewell, My Wallace

by Bob Mosher and Joe Connelly in the manner of
Raymond Chandler

(Eddie narrates)

My office that year was above a fire station. I figured it would be the last place my parents would look for me. You see, they were hell-bent on talking me out of being a private dick. But 1 was determined to stick with it, even if it meant looking down the wrong end of a parent's throat now and then.

Gus the Fireman ran the station. He'd come up to the office on occasion and talk about the baseball scores. Then he'd try to talk me out of being a gumshoe, and I'd sap him.

And then my first client walked in. I'd been sitting on the floor beating out a tattoo on my bongos, so the first thing 1 saw was a pair of ankles propped up on high heels. 1 lifted my eyes slowly, and the body under that dress threw me one curve after another. By the time my eyes finally got to her face, though, I knew I'd struck out. It was Mrs. Cleaver.

I leaped to my feet and said, "Good afternoon, Mrs. Cleaver. Lovely day, isn't it?" The eyes that looked back at me were round and liquidy, as if they'd spent too much time gazing into pots. She said, "Why, Eddie, don't you think you should give up being a shamus and go back to your parents?" I countered with, "Why don't you sit down and tell me what's really on your mind?"

I hit the nail right on the head because she slumped into a chair and said, "It's about Wally." I said, "Wallace? Wallace Cleaver? Tell me all about it." She said, "I'm worried about him. He's—he's—" I said, "Has he disappeared?" She said, "Now why would you say such a thing, Eddie? You were at the house visiting Wally just last night." I gave her that apologetic look you've seen me pull on so many episodes, the one that always fools them. She said, "No, Eddie. It's not his body that's disappeared. It's his ... personality."

I got out my scratch pad and drew some doodads on it to cover up her embarrassment. After a while I said, "When did you last see his personality, Mrs. Cleaver?" She thought about it for a minute and her eyes got troubled like soup boiling over in a pot. At length she said, "Not since the first season." I said, "And you've waited this long to get help?" She nearly broke into tears, but not quite, of course, and said, "I'd hoped he'd turn out like other boys, Eddie. But I've finally realized that he's only a cardboard burlesque of American teenagehood." I promised her that I'd do what I could and told her to take the air, but not in those words. When she had left, I got my office malt out of my desk and took a shot to brace myself.

It wasn't a tough case to break when you got right down to it. That afternoon I went to the Cleaver house and received permission to look around. I turned up Wally's personality right away. It was behind a bookshelf in his father's den. Years of getting lectured to in there about all the things a boy shouldn't do had shriveled it up until it had finally dropped right off Wally's body like a discarded snakeskin. But what did it matter where your personality went once you'd lost it? I thought. You were cardboard, you were missing the big dimension, the third one. You didn't care about the sterility anymore. Me, I was part of the sterility now. I let myself out of the Cleaver house and stood on the steps. It was a cool day and very clear. You could see a long way—but not as far as Wally's personality had gone.

Just then my parents jumped out from behind the rosebushes and grabbed me. I managed to sap my old man, but then my mom got her nails into me. Then the lawn opened up in front of me, and I was falling into a pool of darkness.

Tag: Beaver, with a quizzical look on his face, is watching Wally do his homework. He says, "Wally, what's it like not having a personality?" Wally says, "Gee, Beav, you should know. You don't have one either." In the pillow fight that ensues, the boys' faces are unmarred by character lines.

June 18–26, 1963

Although Ken Osmond was ecstatic about playing a tough guy instead of a wise guy for once, little near-albino Stanley Fafara was offended that lower forms of literature were being considered for the series.

Next, Gomalco received composer John Cage's avant-garde interpretation of the *Beaver* theme, in which the musical notes are spaced thirty seconds apart and run through the entire episode. Doddering Pablo Picasso contributed a design for the boys' bedroom in which he rehashed his favorite motifs of the preceding forty years. The flow of scripts continued: Ira Levin's *June's Baby,* Kobo Abe's *Beaver in the Dunes,* Norman Mailer's *The Beaver and the Dead,* Harlan Ellison's *I Have No Beaver But I Must Scream,* and Franz Kafka's *Beavermorphosis,* as imagined by his friend and biographer, Max Brod.

Beavermorphosis

by Max Brod in the manner of
Franz Kafka

Theodore Cleaver awakes one morning to find he has become a giant beaver. Young W awakes, sees him, and says, "Gee, Beav, I always knew you were a goof, but I didn't know you were that big a goof. Boy oh boy, wait'll Dad sees this." T slaps his tail on the sheets in protest.

At breakfast, old W, young W, and J eat scrambled eggs. T gnaws the table legs. J says, "Beaver, I told you to stop that."

On the way to school T dams up a stream running through M's Field. His friend G, who happens to be standing nearby, says, "Boy, Beav, you're really gonna get it now." T slaps his tail in terror and flees. A dogcatcher chases him, but he reaches home and hides.

Mrs. R, the school principal, comes to the house to speak to J. Young W answers the door. He searches for, but cannot find, J. Mrs. R departs. When J returns, young W gives her the message. She calls old W at work but cannot reach him.

Meanwhile T has climbed a tree. He falls into a large soup bowl. Unable to escape, he slaps his tail against the sides in anxiety. Inexplicably, his friend WW happens to have been watching from below and calls, "Boy, Beav, you're really gonna get it now."

Old W receives J's message and goes to GA Grammar School. He is unable to find Mrs. R. But as he emerges from the building, a man in a gray suit serves him a subpoena.

Tag: T has returned to human form. In bed, he asks young W, "Wally, do you think Dad'll ever know why he's on trial?" Young W says, "Search me, Beav. I'll never understand grown-ups." They plump up their pillows and roll over. Young W turns out the light, but the room remains preternaturally bright.

June 26–30, 1963

On the heels of other noteworthy musical contributions, a reel of audiotape arrived containing a version of the *Beaver* theme with an original set of lyrics. Although the envelope in which it came was lost, it took no time for everyone at Gomalco to realize that it had to be the work of felonious country baritone Johnny Cash.

> *I'm stuck in Mayfield Prison, yeah,*
> *And time keeps marchin' on.*
> *I wish there was a train to blow,*
> *But where would it come from?*
> *Daddy named me*
> *Beaver so I would fight,*
> *I hate gir-uls*
> *But hittin' them ain't right.*
> *I'm stuck in Mayfield Prison, yeah,*
> *And time keeps passin' by,*
> *I punched a squirt in Metzger's Field*
> *So I could watch him cry.*

While the cast mulled over this new contribution, a script arrived from a successful television writer.

The Beaver Zone

Rod Serling

(Joe Connelly stands before the camera, narrating.) Identity is a funny thing. Case in point Mr. Ward B. Cleaver. He doesn't know who he is. But he doesn't think it's funny. Hence the paradox of our little story tonight as we follow Mr. Cleaver along the road that leads both in and out of...the Beaver Zone.

The Cleavers are having dinner. June says, "And what did you do today, Wally?" Wally: "Well, me and Eddie Haskell walked past the girls' basketball court and Eddie started making funny noises." Ward: "Now why would Eddie want to do that?" Beaver: "Because he's a creep." Wally crinkles his pug nose in a cute smile.

A voice offstage yells, "Cut." Everybody darts from the table except Ward, who gazes about in bewilderment. Director Norman Abbot says, "You did pretty well, Hugh." Ward looks offstage, sees lights and cameras, and says, "What's going on here?" Jerry Mathers, smoking a cigarette offstage, says, "Quit screwin' around, Beaumont. We gotta film the scene where Larry falls into the cesspool."

Ward slams his hand down on the table and yells, "Beaver, how can you say such a thing?" Barbara Billingsley says, "Christ, the old lush is at it again." Bob

Mosher, the coproducer, looks at Ward sympathetically and says, "Come on, Hugh. Let's go down a couple." Ward, in consternation, cries, "Why are you calling me Hugh? My name is Ward. Ward Cleaver. This is my family—June, Wally, and the Beaver." The entire cast laughs derisively.

Mosher gently leads Ward out of the studio, onto the streets of Burbank, California. Ward says, "This isn't Mayfield. Where are we?" Tony Dow follows them outside and yells after Mosher, "Hey, Bob. When we gonna do another episode with Miss Landers? That dish gives me the hots." Ward, with a look of utter horror, yells, "Wally!" Dow says, "Not bad, Hugh. You'll have me believing it myself pretty soon." He laughs coarsely and returns indoors. Mosher glances worriedly at Ward and says, "I forgot something, Hugh. I'll be right back." He follows Dow.

Ward, left alone, runs down the street accosting strangers, saying, "This isn't Mayfield. How do I get to Mayfield?" One replies, "Mayfield? Is that in California?" Ward: "No, no. It's in— it's in—"

Mosher reappears. He finds Ward standing by himself in the middle of the traffic-congested street, saying, "It's— it's—it's in—" Mosher, leading him back to the curb, says, "Hugh, I thought you promised this wouldn't happen again. There are other actors out there, you know: John Forsythe, Robert Young, Carl Betz." Ward says, "I'm not an actor, I work in an office with Fred Rutherford. I was in the Seabees during the war. I used to walk twenty miles to school every day. What kind of game is this? Why do you want me to think I'm some actor named—"

Ward suddenly breaks off and says, "Wait a minute. I don't know you. Who are you?" Mosher: "Come on, Hugh.

You want to go back to making pictures like *The Mole People?*"

Ward wheels about and runs off. He comes to a train station. He boards a commuter train. Exhausted by his ordeal, he falls asleep. The next thing he knows, the conductor's voice is calling, "Mayfield, Mayfield." After a moment of uncertainty, he leaps off the train as it pulls away from the station. June, Wally, and the Beaver are waiting for him, smiling cutely. June says, "Hello, dear. We've been waiting for you." She takes his arm, and the family leads him off along the sun-dappled streets of Mayfield.

Tag: Beaver is looking out of the boys' bedroom window. He sees Bob Mosher standing on the street corner. He says, "Look, Wally. There's that strange man who's been hounding Dad." Just then Mosher glances up at the window. Wally says, "We'd better turn off the light, Beav." He does, but the room remains eerily lit.

July 1–7, 1963

Fear of the show's imminent cancellation swept through the acting community, and a mass of actors suddenly petitioned to appear on *Leave It to Beaver*. Such luminaries as Gregory Peck, Sir Ralph Richardson, George Gobel, Katharine Hepburn, James Cagney, Paul Lynde, Tina Louise, Bob Mitchum, Lillian Gish, and Eva Gabor demanded to play friends and neighbors of the Cleavers.

Perhaps stirred by this celebrity attention, then-President John F. Kennedy pledged, in an Independence Day address to the nation, "By the end of this decade, America will better understand itself and its place in the world. The Cleavers will be broadcast to the depths of the oceans, to the outer reaches of the universe, and behind the iron curtain. Ask not what *Leave It to Beaver* can do for you, but what you can do for *Leave It to Beaver*."

From Greenwich Village, world-renowned mythologist and resentful ex-Catholic Joseph Campbell announced the commencement of a new project, *The Beaver with a Thousand Faces,* a massive study of the figure of the silly child throughout the world's mythologies. Campbell explained, "Through Theodore Cleaver, modern man can live again the one eternally ineffable, shape-shifting myth of the cute little boy who grows into a gawky, big-headed teenager."

Composer Aaron Copland and choreographer Agnes De Mille visited the set to discuss the possibility of staging *Beaver the Kid,* a self-consciously American ballet episode.

That same day, in the mail arrived Larry McMurtry's *Beaver Pass By,* Vladimir Nabokov's *Pale Beaver,* Mickey Spillane's *I, the Beaver,* and a script by regular writers Conway and MacLane, who also wanted to get in on the dead-authors act. This last script was tentatively put on the docket for the 1963-1964 season.

Lady Cleaver's Beaver

by Dick Conway and Roland MacLane in the manner of
D.H. Lawrence

Beaver comes into the kitchen where June is frosting a cake. He says, "Hey, Mom. Can I ask you something?" June: "Why of course, Beaver." Beaver: "Well, there's this new kid in class and whenever Miss Landers reads the roll and comes to his name she giggles and blushes." June says, "Why, that's strange. What's the boy's name?" Beaver says, "John Thomas," and June giggles and blushes.

Beaver says, "Gee, Mom. You did it, too. What's so funny about John Thomas?" June: "Why, Beaver. Don't you know what John Thomas means? I thought Wally would have explained it to you." When Beaver still looks perplexed, screwing on his cap at different angles, June says, "That means your little pogo stick, Beaver." Still getting no reaction, June adds, "You know, Beaver. Your piccolo. Your exhaust pipe. Your great white root. Your tower of power."

Beaver: "Gee, Mom. Those things sound like a lot of different junk to me. John Thomas doesn't look like any of them." At the mention of the name, June giggles and blushes. Beaver: "Gee Mom." June, growing more intense and gesturing toward his groin, says, "Come now, Beaver. Your pink chimney. Your veined monument. Your Tom Johnson. Your beaver cleaver."

Beaver: "Gee, Mom. You mean it's the same name as mine?" June, rolling her eyes up in her head and batting her lashes furiously, says, "No, no, no, Theodore. You know, you must have played with it." Beaver: "Sure, Mom. We played softball today." "No, Beaver. Not playing with him. Playing with it. Like plucking the staff. Like rubbing the nub. Like rolling the dough. Like bruising the fruit."

Beaver: "Gee, Mom." June says, "Beaver, you must know. John Thomas means cock. Prick. Dick. Dong. Wang. Slab. Dink. Rod. Shaft. Tool. Meat. Poomba. Prong. Joint. Hog. Choda. Penis. You understand now, Beaver?"

Beaver: "Gee, Mom. One kid sure has a lot of names." June, in a fit of fury, tears Beaver's pants open and points at that which makes him a man. She says, "That, Beaver, that. What in the world do you boys call it?" Beaver: "Gee, Mom. Me and the guys never talk about it." June, straightening up and getting that thoughtful look in her eyes, says, "That's odd, Beaver. Neither does your father."

Tag: Wally is combing his hair in front of the mirror. Beaver says, "Hey, Wally. Where are you going?" Wally: "I'm taking Mary Ellen Rogers to the movies." Beaver: "And after that?" Wally: "Gee, probably get a malt, I guess." Beaver: "And after that?" Wally: "Gee, take her home, I guess." Beaver: "And after that?" Wally: "Gosh, Beav. What would we do then?" Beaver: "I don't know. I thought maybe you'd make a two-backed beast." Wally says, "Aw, where do you get those goofy ideas?" and throws a pillow at him.

July 7–10, 1963

When Barbara Billingsley was asked what she thought of her role in the script, she blushed and giggled. Beaumont smiled and patted her arm affectionately. Mathers spent the afternoon consulting his dictionary. Only little blanched Stanley Fafara seemed displeased. When asked to comment, he made a pornographic gesture with his fingers and buried his nose in *The Plumed Serpent.*

Tony Dow was angered by rumors that singer Fabian sought to replace him as Wally on the show. This rumor, unlike those that came later, turned out to be groundless.

Killjoy French philosopher Jean-Paul Sartre telephoned Hugh Beaumont, his old beer-drinking friend from the days of the Resistance, to discuss his new project, *Beaver and Nothingness.* Sartre reported that watching episodes of *Leave It to Beaver* filled him with nausea. After hanging up, Beaumont was heard to ask, "Now why on earth would J. P. write a book about something that made him sick?"

On July 10, a then little-known group of young English musicians called the Beatles sent in their own version of the *Beaver* theme song. Unfortunately, sole surviving copyright holder Paul McCartney, best known for his romance with Jane Asher, refused to release the lyrics for publication.

Although it cannot be certified, many claim that the young Rolling Stones wrote a version of their own shortly after, but Keith Richard accidentally burned it while heating a spoon.

Meanwhile, the ABC executives, dismayed after placing poorly in the golf tournament, were in no condition to arrive at a decision on the cancellation of *Beaver*.

Other scripts received included: *Naked Beaver* by William Burroughs, *What Makes Beaver Run?* by Budd Schulberg, Thomas Malory's *Le Morte de Beaver* as conceived by T. H. White, and, from as far as Africa, Chinua Achebe's *Beavers Fall Apart*.

Here follows bilingual absurdist Samuel Beckett's drama of intellectual atrophy.

Waiting for Wally

Samuel Beckett

SCENE:

EDDIE *and* LUMPY *are waiting for Wally under a bare tree in Metzger's Field.*

LUMPY. What do you want to do until Wally gets here?

EDDIE. Nothing.

LUMPY. Okay. *(Long silence)* Hey, Eddie, how do you do that?

(EDDIE *abruptly pulls off* LUMPY'S *letterman sweater and cuts out the two letters. He attempts to spell various words, but as both letters are identical, his choices are limited.*)

LUMPY. Hey, Eddie, what are you spelling?

EDDIE. Nothing.

LUMPY *(thoughtfully)*. Gosh, don't you need an N to spell Nothing?

(EDDIE *inexplicably seizes* LUMPY *and endeavors to push him through a knothole in the tree.*)

(WHITEY *enters with* LARRY *on a leash.* WHITEY *is dressed like Liberace.*)

WHITEY. Do either of you gentlemen want to buy a boy?

EDDIE and LUMPY. No. We want nothing.

WHITEY. The price is reasonable, especially when you consider his great virtue. He can eat. (*He punches* LARRY *in the stomach*) Eat!

(LARRY *rapidly eats a melon, six Cornish hens, a rhubarb pie, forty-nine chilies, a side of beef, an anchovy pizza, a loaf of bread, six haddocks, a can of Alpo, seven Tootsie Rolls, a pound of butter, a box of Wheaties, fourteen heads of lettuce, and an apple. The three others gut-punch him until he stops.* WHITEY *and* LARRY *exit.*)

LUMPY. Hey, Eddie, what'll Wally do for you when he comes?

EDDIE. Nothing.

LUMPY. And what'll he do for me when he comes?

EDDIE. Nothing.

LUMPY. Oh, boy. I knew old Wally would come through.

(EDDIE *suddenly draws into a ball and begins screaming.* LUMPY *watches him reflectively.*)

LUMPY. Hey, Eddie, what are you going to major in at State?

EDDIE. Nothing.

LUMPY. What are you going to do when you grow up?

EDDIE. Nothing.

LUMPY. Boy, Eddie, you've sure got it made.

(WHITEY *and* LARRY *return from the opposite direction.* WHITEY *is sunburned and* LARRY *is paralyzed in the throat.* LARRY *leads* WHITEY *offstage.*)

LUMPY. Eddie, what am I?

EDDIE. Nothing.

LUMPY. Gosh, that's funny. That's what my daddy always says.

(*Long silence. EDDIE beats his head rhythmically against the tree. BEAVER enters, dressed like Elvis Presley.*)

BEAVER. Hey, creeps, Wally says he isn't coming today. Wait for him tomorrow.

(EDDIE *and* LUMPY *attempt suicide by leaping up in the air and twisting their bodies so that they land on their heads. Failing that, they sit and wait.*)

Tag: BEAVER *sits waiting for Wally in their room under a bare pennant. He speaks French and studies the wall with a telescope. When Wally fails to arrive he hits himself with a pillow and goes to bed.*

July 11, 1963

On a hot, historic night in July, Jerry Mathers was a guest on *The Tonight Show* starring a young Johnny Carson.

Carson: "Is it true, Jerry, that *Leave It to Beaver* has become the focal point of the world's eye?" Mathers: "Yeah. I just wish it had happened when I was a cute little kid, before my head outgrew my body and turned me into a bucktoothed creep." McMahon: "Hey-o!!!"

Meanwhile, Mosher and Connelly, with the assistance of multitalented Hugh Beaumont, had completed their second homage to a departed author.

Beaverwolf

by Bob Mosher, Joe Connelly, and Hugh Beaumont
in the manner of

Hermann Hesse

Beaver is walking home from school, humming *In the Hall of the Mountain King*. He glances down a side street and glimpses a sign that reads FOR BEAVERS ONLY. He does a double take, but the sign has vanished. He mutters, "Gee," under his breath.

Awestruck, he goes and sits by the creek where he produces a reed pipe on which he plays *In the Hall of the Mountain King*. By and by, he puts the pipe away and contemplates the water. In a flash of insight, he realizes that the way to Nirvana is an eightfold path strewn with various right turns. Unfortunately, he doesn't know what Nirvana means. He makes a mental note to ask Ward about it, but just then Larry chances by. They play grab-ass for a while and Beaver forgets all about his insight.

When he gets home he finds Wally and Eddie in the bedroom playing the glass bead game. Eddie says, "Hey, squirt." Beaver asks them how the game is played and Eddie says, "Get with it, kid. Or do you want to fall prey to the fragmentation and dilettantism of twentieth-century life?" Wally says, "Lay off him, Eddie." Beaver says, "Yeah."

But Beaver feels despondent. As always when he encounters Eddie, he realizes that, at heart, he is an outsider, that he is torn between his ideals and the real, objective world. How can he endure school and family life when all his dreams revolve around having milk and cookies and playing grab-ass? He decides that modern technology is to blame, but sadly, he doesn't know what technology means.

June has cooked a pot roast that evening and Beaver, wolfing his food, forgets to ask Ward the meaning of technology. But, as if he has subconsciously recognized the roots of his anguish, he sneaks out of the house that night and dumps his bike in Miller's Pond. Walking home, he happens to glance down the same side street he did before and spots the cryptic sign again. In another flash of insight, he realizes that in order to relate to humanity he must overcome his sexual taboos. Tragically, he doesn't know what taboo or, for that matter, sexual means. He shrugs it off and runs home, playing grab-ass with himself.

Tag: The boys are getting ready for bed. Beaver asks Wally, "What does *Zerrissenheit* mean?" Wally says, "*Zerrissenheit* means disintegration, particularly in reference to the character of artists. I just learned that in my German class." Beaver says, "Thanks, Wally." Wally turns off the light, but it makes little, if any, difference to the room's luminosity.

July 12–20, 1963

One would think that the next surprise would be a pleasant one, considering Beaumont's lifelong admiration of Sir Laurence Olivier. Beaumont was the first to welcome Olivier's request to appear on the show. But when the venerable Englishman, not satisfied with a guest appearance, sought to take over the role of Ward, Beaumont was miffed. "I'm sure Sir Laurence is a much better actor than I," he said. "I would have a great deal of difficulty, for example, playing Hamlet. But we're a family here. Can mere acting virtuosity triumph over the real paternal feelings I have for Beaver and Wally? I mean, for Jerry and Tony?"

Olivier took his plea to the ABC executives. For once, they seemed impressed.

Gastronomic pop artist Claes Oldenburg delivered the new furniture he designed for the Cleavers to Gomalco Productions' offices. Among the pieces were a desk in the shape of a hamburger, beds in the shape of malts, and a wall pennant in the shape of a croissant. Hugh Beaumont was particularly tickled by the golf clubs that looked like a bag of french fries.

The second shot fired in the political war building over *Leave It to Beaver* was former Vice President Richard Milhous Nixon's rebuttal to Kennedy's Fourth of July speech. "As usual, the intellectual elite is trying to undermine a

fundamental American tradition. This invasion of an
American institution by foreigners and misfits is the direct
result of this administration's pink-tinted policies. The talk
of renaissance we hear from the campus hotbeds of
creeping socialism is no more than delusions of grandeur."

Synchronicities abound. The day after Nixon's speech,
a teleplay by dedicated police-booster and Red-baiter Jack
Webb arrived.

Red Beaver
Jack Webb

SATURDAY. 8:32 A.M.

Ward awakes and finds the room slightly changed. The blurry painting of a street in Paris—or Venice, perhaps—has been replaced by a photograph of a mechanized dairy. When he turns on the tap he sees a suspect greenish froth in the water and decides not to brush his teeth.

8:56 A.M.

Downstairs, he finds June setting the breakfast table with austere iron plates. She says, "Good morning, Comrade," and pecks him on the cheek. Beaver enters, sternly says, "Good morning, Comrade Parents," and sits down. June and Beaver eat their barley mush in silence. Ward says, "But where's Wally?" Beaver says coolly, "Gee, don't you remember, Comrade Father? Comrade Wallace was transferred." Ward grows worried, asking, "Transferred? Beaver, what—" Beaver and June gasp in horror. June throws her hand over Ward's mouth. She says, "Please! There are no bourgeois rodent names in this household. Isn't that right, Comrade Theodore?" Beaver says, "The state would not permit revanchist rodent names." He adds in a whisper, "Gee, Dad. Do you want to get me sent to the camp?"

9:28 A.M.

Ward goes to the closet. He finds his golf clubs replaced by a hammer and a sickle. He begins to ask, "June, have you seen my—" when Beaver marches by in uniform. Beaver says, "Good day, Comrade Father. It is my time to go to school." Ward says, "Beav— Theodore, you don't go to school on Saturday." Beaver says, very loudly, as if someone is listening, "I go to the General People's Moral and Mechanical School from nine-forty-five a.m. until seven-forty-five p.m. every Saturday. I have a perfect record of attendance and blind obedience. I have no desires other than to drive a tractor and serve the State." He adds, "And besides, Larry Mondello's been condemned as a capitalist pig, and me and all the guys get to punch him in the stomach." He adjusts his helmet several different ways and leaves the house.

9:34 A.M.

Ward is about to leave and follow him when Eddie Haskell appears at the front door in a fur cap and heavy overcoat. "Good morning, Comrade Cleaver. I have come here to discuss your son, Comrade Wallace." Impatiently, Ward says, "Wally isn't here right now, Eddie. And I don't have time to talk to you." Eddie says, "It would be expedient for you to make time, Tovarisch Cleaver. That means it would be smart. Unless, of course, you want to explain yourself to the Purification Board. As Security Marshall of Maydayfield, that is in my power, as you should have learned from the case of Comrade Rutherford. I believe his bald skull is still on view on the pike in Metzger's Field."

9:41 A.M.

Wally appears in a dark uniform, toting a submachine gun. Eddie greets him, "Whadaya say, Comrade Gertrude? People's Kindergarten out so soon?" He laughs mechanically. Wally says, "Aw, cut it out, Comrade Haskell. I have been duly processed and made a joyful slave of the State. Now I only need to exterminate an enemy of the people and I will be granted a letter on my uniform." Ward cries out, "Wally, what is this? This is madness!" Eddie grins maliciously and says, "Behold, Tovarisch. An enemy of the people." Ward screams, "I'm not your enemy! Wally, I'm your father!" Wally cuts his father to ribbons with machine-gun fire.

SATURDAY. 8:32 a.m.

Ward awakes, screaming, in bed. He looks around. He sees the blurry picture of a street in Paris—or Venice, perhaps. He runs downstairs and looks in the closet. Realizing that it was only a nightmare, he leaps through the house, swinging his five iron like a club, crying, "Seabees forever!"

Tag: 9:17 p.m. The boys are huddled in their room. Beaver says, "Gee, Wally, do you think the Commies are coming to Mayfield like Dad says?" Wally says, "I dunno, Beav, but the sooner he gets the house moved into the bomb shelter, the calmer I'll feel." He turns out the light, but the searchlights in the yard keep the room safely lit.

July 21–25, 1963

Ironically, it was Webb's script that brought the ABC executives out of their cloud of apathy and reluctance. They announced, "If this level of timely, significant thought continues, we might see our way clear to keeping *Beaver* on the air."

During the cast party that followed, it was learned that the four principals were to appear simultaneously on the covers of *Time* and *Newsweek* magazines. In its editorial, *Time* explained, "For their service as a solid pillar of American culture, *Time* has selected the Cleavers as Family of the Year." In contrast, *Newsweek* wrote, "For their contribution as a firm column of American society, *Newsweek* honors the Cleavers as the Family of 1963."

Little bleached Stanley Fafara objected, "Literary purity is invariably corrupted by governmental associations." But the producers were thrilled. Mosher noted, "Me and Joe, we were sure happy to see our kids on those covers. Hot dog, especially if it keeps the Reds off our shores." Supermammarian Italian actress Sophia Loren showed up at the Gomalco offices to argue with Barbara Billingsley about usurping the role of June. Unable to gain Barbara's agreement, she pledged to take her demand to ABC executives.

"I know she's attractive," said Barbara, desperately clutching her housedress to her breast, "but can you imagine the extremes a woman with a Latin temper like that would go to in disciplining the boys?"

Dow and Mathers looked vaguely disappointed.

After lunch that day members of the cast found Ken Osmond sitting in the Cleaver living-room set, strumming a guitar and playing a harmonica. Frank "Lumpy Rutherford" Bank was singing a song, which, they shortly learned, was the contribution of a freewheeling folk singer who signed his name only as "Dylan." Like Johnny Cash's earlier submission, the words were meant to be sung to the *Beaver* theme.

> *There is a fam'ly in Nowhereland,*
> *Livin' on God's right hand.*
> *So much virtue is kinda strange,*
> *I wonder if times will change.*
> *June is pretty*
> *Just like a woman is.*
> *Ward is headstrong,*
> *The last word is always his.*
> *There is a family steeped in lore,*
> *They're knockin' on Heaven's door.*
> *Heed these words, you masters of war,*
> *Or you will be no more.*

The entire cast was amazed at the ability of a Welsh poet to write a song in such a convincing American folk idiom.

Scripts that came in that afternoon included Saul Bellow's *Seize the Beaver,* Graham Greene's *The Beaver and the Glory,* and young Ken Kesey's *Sometimes a Great Beaver.* Interestingly enough, the Kesey script, which related the life of an errant, third Cleaver child, showed striking parallels to the teleplay submitted that week by critic Malcolm Cowley: a drama of Southern reprobates by the late Nobel-Prize winning dirt farmer William Faulkner.*

*Originally it was believed that Cowley had written the script in the manner of Faulkner, who had died a year before. However, subsequent diligent research—specifically, reading Cowley's cover letter, which had gotten stuck in the envelope when the script was originally pulled out—has revealed that the script is, in fact, the work of the lion of Rowan Oak himself. It seems that Faulkner had become fascinated with *Leave It to Beaver* while wasting away in the sanitarium at Byhalia, Mississippi, either because he saw in it a family saga to rival in breadth and complexity his own tales of Yoknapatawpha County, or because the sanitarium's TV reception was too weak to pick up *The Defenders.* So distraught was he after watching the final episode of the fifth season, dreading the long, hot summer with no *Beaver,* that he began to write his own series of episodes. Tragically, death came for the great novelist just six days later, hours after completing this first script's tag.

The Beaver and the Fury
William Faulkner

Wally stands in front of the old, rotting school with a group of students. Lumper Rutherford asks, "Did you hear that Eddie Haskell has nigger blood in him?" Wally says, "They say he was an orphan before he was a son." Lumper says, "That's probably where he gets his curly hair." Just then Eddie appears, a cigarette slanting from his chin, his face the queer bloodless color of stamped tin. He says to Wally, "Hey, Sam, want to help me steal some mules tonight?" Wally says, "That is neither adjunctive nor incremental to the forwarding of my design." Lumper says, "Hey, Eddie, I hear you're a nigger." Eddie says, "If you don't shut your mouth, I'll drill a hole in your coffin when you die."

Wally says, "Ain't it true, Eddie, that you came out of nowhere and without warning, upon the land with a band of strange niggers, and begot, in repudiation, a son before you yourself were begotten?" Eddie replies, "You're one to talk. I hear your sister lost her virginity to a Slopes." Lumper says, "Gosh, Wally, I didn't know you had a sister."

Eddie says, "Yeah, Hibiscus Cleaver. She lost it in a rhubarb patch with Sputum Slopes and left for Europe. And then there was Sparkle Cleaver. He got the cow-clap from a heifer and it went to his head. Not to mention Gibbon

Cleaver. He thought he was a fish and drowned himself in Miller's Pond. And last but not least, Weevil Cleaver, who got in a sickle fight with Bark Buffrin and lost the capacity to pass on the Cleaver name."

Undismayed, Wally says, "It's just as well, ain't it, Eddie, that as if in repudiation of the Cleaver name that he could no longer pass on, he forsook this postbellum land, where women haunt the sick, fevered soil like ghosts, and again, in repudiation of the very forefathers who stamped their blind, retrograde destiny on this dry postage stamp of a country, he went off and became a caddy up at the country club?" When Wally says, "caddy," Lumper begins bellerin'.

That night, a group of boys burn down Eddie Haskell's house. Everyone escapes except the widow.

Tag: Beaver is in the bedroom. Wally is in the mirror. From downstairs we hear the chuck-chuck-chuck of an adze. Beaver asks, "Hey Wally, is Mom a fish?" Wally, no longer in the mirror, hits him with a pillow and breaks his watch.

July 25–28, 1963

Although most of the cast was very pleased with Faulkner's work, they were all a little despondent over the death of the widow. Richard "Fred Rutherford" Deacon, outraged that death should come to Mayfield, wanted to lynch Mr. Faulkner, but Hugh Beaumont mollified him.

As if to thicken the murk of morbidity, Billy Graham, evangelist and proponent of joyous death, took the pulpit at the Disneyland Hotel in Anaheim to condemn "this putrid corruption of a once-healthy body of American morality." Blind to practical considerations, he called for a return to the classic *Beaver* tradition. "God came down to me," he hollered, "and He said to me, 'Billy, you must lead the eyes of Christians back to the Cleavers of yore and away from this modern Mayfield and Gomorrah where an Eddie Haskell can triumph in his scarlet worldly schemes.'"

Little albuminous Stanley Fafara, inspired by Sinclair Lewis, pelted him with eggs from the audience, spoiling Brother Graham's new five-hundred-dollar suit.

As if in defiance of Graham's admonitions, the world continued heaping its accolades on Gomalco when jazz magazine *Downbeat* showcased Pete Rugolo, who, in the most recent season of *Beaver,* had added his own jazz touch to Dave Kahn's original theme music. Featured both on the cover sporting wraparound shades and in an interview, Rugolo was quoted as saying, "Me and Bird were tight. Named my dog Bird. Man's gotta blow his ax, dig? Newport, Montreux, Blackhawk. What's the meaning of the blues, Daddy-O? It's groovin' in the summertime, gettin' cool. Cat's gotta scheme."

In the continuing influx of artistic contributions, Spanish surrealist Salvador Dali, always trying to be different, submitted not a set design but a wax moustache for Ward. Beaumont tried it on and everyone laughed.

Two scripts arrived. The first was the victim of a tragic misunderstanding: Misreading the cover letter, Mosher and Connelly took it to be *The Secret Life of Beaver Cleaver* by James Thurber. Noting its dependence on broad gags, ludicrous teen slang, and preposterous plot complications, they dismissed it as the work of a snobbish Thurber writing down to the sitcom medium. Subsequent diligent research— namely, holding the coffee-stained cover letter up to a bright light—has revealed that the script was, in fact, *The Many Loves of Beaver Cleaver,* by Max Shulman. If they had known that, the producers might have been able to use it to rekindle the interest of ABC executives, especially if they'd followed Shulman's advice for hiring Bob Denver to play a beret-wearing Eddie Haskell and Warren Beatty to bring a new sexual intensity to Lumpy Rutherford.

As it turned out, however, all their attention went to Walter Kaufmann's philosophical poem-drama based on the works of mustachioed syphilitic philologist Friedrich Nietzsche.

Thus Spake Beaver

by Walter Kaufmann in the manner of

Friedrich Nietzsche

When Beaver was fourteen years old he left his home and the pond of his home and went up to the lake. Here he enjoyed his milk and his cookies and for ten hours he did not tire of them. But at last a change came over his stomach, and one morning he descended alone from the lake. He encountered no one at first, but when he came into the Cleaver kitchen, all at once there sat before him his family at the breakfast table.

And thus spake Beaver to his family:

"Behold, this cup has become empty again and Beaver wants milk again."

Beaver descended alone from the breakfast table, encountering no one, but when he came to the front door, all at once there stood his mother before him, who gave him his lunch pail.

And thus spake Beaver to his mother:

"The idealist is incorrigible: If he is thrown out of his house, he makes an ideal of his school."

Beaver walked alone to school, encountering no one, but when he came into the hall, all at once there stood before him Larry Mondello, who bit into an apple.

And thus spake Beaver to Larry Mondello:

"Shared cookies make a friend, not getting in trouble together," and he punched Larry Mondello in the stomach.

Beaver walked alone into the classroom, encountering no one, but when he took his seat, all at once there stood before him Miss Landers, calling his name in roll.

And thus spake Beaver to Miss Landers:

"The surest way to corrupt a young man is to teach him to esteem more highly those who think differently than those who think alike."

Beaver descended alone from school, encountering no one, but when he walked into the fire station, all at once there slumped before him on his stool Gus the Fireman.

And thus spake Beaver to Gus the Fireman:

"In disrespecting, we show that we still maintain a sense of respect," and he spat on Gus the Fireman.

Beaver descended alone from the fire station, encountering no one, and when he arrived at the bridge, all at once there stood no one before him, and so he spat off the bridge.

And thus spake Beaver to no one:

"A child would rather have the void for his purpose than be void of spit."

Beaver descended alone from the bridge, encountering no one, and when he drew near to his house, all at once there stood before him Eddie Haskell, and Eddie Haskell gave him the business.

And thus spake Beaver to Eddie Haskell:

"That which does not destroy me makes you creepier."

Beaver entered alone into the house, encountering no one, and when he tried to sneak up to his room, all at once his father yelled his name, and his father lectured him.

And thus spake Beaver to his father:

"Forgive us our virtues, that is what we should ask of our viewers."

Tag: Beaver ascended alone to his bedroom, encountering no one, and when he opened the door, all at once there sat his brother before him doing his homework.

And thus spake Beaver to his brother:

"When one has not had a good father, one must become a child actor."

And having spake thus, Beaver crawled into bed and turned off the light, but the room glowed as strong as a morning sun that comes out of dark mountains.

July 29–August 4, 1963

Beaumont's only comment on the script was "I wish I'd kept that moustache from the Spanish fellow. I could have lent it to Jerry and made his performance more believable."

The executives were unavailable for discussion due to a series of luncheons. As July turned to August, the cast tried to keep busy playing badminton and organizing a softball game on the Metzger's Field set.

Because of the mimeographed scripts that innumerable periodicals had received, the first reviews of the unproduced episodes began arriving at Gomalco.

"Terrific."—Rex Reed

"Profoundly American."—*Saturday Review*

"A Dazzling Tour de Force."—*San Francisco Chronicle*

"As if John Dos Passos had written *Madame Bovary*."—*New York Review of Books*

"As if Jack Kerouac had written *Leave It to Beaver*."—*L.A. Herald-Examiner*

"Makes you glad to be human."—Kirkus Reviews

"Makes rodents glad to be human."—Cleveland Amory

"This year's *Lost Horizon*."—*Modesto Bee*

"Has the tang of a vintage sherry."—*Times Literary Supplement*

"Scintillating."—Rona Barrett

"Will take its place beside *Grand Illusion and The Honeymooners*."—*Photoplay*

"Beav Brings Big Brains."—*Variety*

More trouble erupted from the acting community when television bit-actor William Shatner sought to squeeze out Tony Dow as Wally Cleaver. Shatner really couldn't be blamed when one considers that the role of the elder Cleaver son gave him much opportunity for the pompous moralizing that later formed the basis of his career as Captain Kirk on *Star Trek*. Still, Dow wasn't sympathetic. After an hour of heated argument, Shatner appealed his case to ABC executives.

The science-fiction community made another contribution to the swelling body of Beaver lore in a script submitted by Kurt Vonnegut.

Welcome to the Beaverhouse

Kurt Vonnegut

One morning, the man from the Great Equalizer Corporation, with a six-and-a-half-inch member, comes to install a Humanizer into the Cleaver household. Ward, with a five-and-a-quarter-inch member, supervising the installation, says, "Thanks, Fuck-head." The man says, "You're welcome, Shit-nose."

Beaver, with a two-and-a-quarter-inch member, is wading across the rice paddy in Vietnam. A grenade lands between his legs and explodes. He screams and walks into the Cleaver kitchen. He says, "Hey, Mom, where are the cookies?" June, memberless, smoking a cigarette, and reading *Cosmopolitan,* says, "I've got no time to make cookies today." Beaver points at the Humanizer and says, "Gee, Mom, what's that?" June says, "That's a machine to make us more like other people, Beav. I got tired of looking forward to lining shelves and making lemonade." Ward enters wearing a white T-shirt and thongs, drinking a beer. Beaver says, "Gee, Dad, you're home early today." Ward says, "Fuck that shit, I didn't go to work today." Grinning at Beaver, he says, "Just think, you little asshole, you're going to be like other little boys pretty soon."

Just then Wally, with a member the same size as his father's, enters, followed by Eddie with a ten-inch member.

Wally has a six-pack under his arm. Eddie says, "Good afternoon, Mr. Cleaver, Mrs. Cleaver. Your son Wallace tells me that you've finally invested in a Humanizer. Welcome to the club. Now if only the Mondellos and the Rutherfords will purchase one, we can all be like other people." Wally says, "No kidding, Dad. Now I'll finally be able to screw Mary Ellen Rogers."

Beaver is in a dome on the planet Rodamlafart. When the interplanetary zoologists learn of his war accident, they kick him out. He treks across a barren wasteland into the Cleaver living room and hears June say, "It's odd that the Humanizer hasn't had any effect on Beaver." Ward says, "Yes, he still buttons his shirt to the neck, wears a baseball cap, and feels guilty about these trivial problems he creates for himself."

They send for the man from the Great Equalizer Corporation. He attaches electrodes to the Beaver's head and gives him an extra shot from the Humanizer, but Beaver is unchanged. The man says, "I'm sorry, but it looks like he'll be the same two-dimensional mockery of American boyhood forever. I recommend euthanasia." The Cleavers agree, but just then the Humanizer shorts out. Reverting to their old selves, they throw the repairman and his machine out of the house. June dashes to the kitchen to get dinner started.

Tag: The boys are in their room. Beaver says, "Hey, Wally, how come I'm unstuck in time?" Wally says, "I dunno. I guess just because you're a big goof." He hits Beaver with a pillow, and Beaver falls into a giant soup bowl.

August 5–12, 1963

Mosher and Connelly began wondering if they were being forced into a creative bed of Procrustes by competing forces. Connelly opined, "Me and Bob, we started thinking that all this attention was more trouble than it was worth. Moses, think how we felt when those Reds started in." He was referring to a joint statement issued by the leading voices of the Communist bloc, propounding their views of *Leave It to Beaver*.

"Barbaric."—Leonid Brezhnev
"Imperialist propaganda."—Ho Chi Minh
"The baying of capitalist running dogs."—Mao Tse-tung
"Bourgeois decadence."—Gus Hall
"Lying exhaust of the capitalist roaders."—Lin Piao
"Heartwarming."—Nikita Khrushchev

Rumors that Khrushchev's affection for the Cleavers precipitated his fall from power have never been dispelled.

Stirred by this latest furor, the Voice of America called upon Gomalco's resident intellectual elitist, little chalky Stanley Fafara, for an interview. Fafara pontificated, "Politics are beneath me. Governmental concerns place arbitrary boundaries upon mankind. I consider myself a universal man. Let's talk about culture."

Acceding to his wishes, interviewer Edward R. Murrow asked him about the literary validity of *Leave It to Beaver*.

Little Fafara replied, "It's proved itself in the critical eye over the last six years. Frankly, I had my doubts about its long-term artistic potential when Mr. Mosher and Mr. Connelly first approached me with the series concept. But then of course I was only seven years old."

Work increased steadily for Gomalco art director Howard Johnson. Designs for Mayfield edifices poured in from the likes of Le Corbusier, Walter Gropius, Mies van der Rohe, and the U.S. Army Corps of Engineers. Paintings for new interiors arrived from senile Catalonian Joan Miro, sickly patron of transvestism Andy Warhol, and maudlin portraitist Norman Rockwell. Budding LeRoy Nieman proposed a garishly colored montage of a softball game in Metzger's Field. David Siqueiros, affected by the absence of Third World influence in Mayfield, offered to adorn the boys' bedroom with an intentionally hideous reminder of La Raza. Cruelly incisive photographer Richard Avedon asked to execute some seminude portraits of Barbara Billingsley.

"The work load wouldn't be so tough," Johnson said, "if I didn't have to keep up my lawsuit against that restaurant chain for stealing my name."

The pressure on Gomalco increased tremendously with an arrival from the editors of *Reader's Digest* of a huge shipment of classics adaptations. Since their quality level was well below that of other submissions, it is perhaps no tragedy that all of them seem to have been misplaced. Among them were Charles Dickens's *A Tale of Two Cleavers,* Stendhal's *Charterhouse of Mayfield,* Dante's *Divine Sitcom,* Shakespeare's *Tragedy of Haskell, Prince of Creeps,* and Sinclair Lewis's *Leave It to Babbitt.*

A much more respectful updating of a great author arrived from a noted Harvard Mark Twain scholar. This script is built upon unpublished writings from the end of Twain's days—by which time life had left him increasingly bitter, pessimistic, and personally offensive—when he attempted to rewrite one of his own best-loved classics.

The Beaver and the Pauper

by a noted Harvard Mark Twain scholar in the manner of
Mark Twain

In a city in the outside world, on a certain autumn day in the third quarter of the twentieth century, a boy was born to a poor family of the name of Durrell, who did not want him. On the same day, in the ancient suburb of Mayfield, an identical child was born to a middle-class family of the name of Cleaver, who did want him. Still, as they grew, each boy came to believe that he was not happy with his lot, and so it was that when the pauper-boy wandered away from home and found himself in Mayfield, they conspired to exchange clothes.

A few minutes later we find Beaver garlanded with the plumes of normalcy and the pauper tricked out in baseball cap, pristine tennis shoes, and shirt buttoned to the neck.

No sooner has the pauper entered the Cleaver home than he meets with a repast of pot roast and brussels sprouts such as he has never encountered before except on television. Goddamn, this is good, he thinks as he gobbles his food. Later he settles into Beaver's comfortable bed and makes pleasant conversation with Wally. But when he asks, "Hey, got a smoke?" the elder Cleaver boy recoils in horror. "Gosh, Beav, don't you know that's bad?" Christ, thinks the pauper, this guy's a square.

Let us now turn to the true Beaver as he enters the apartment of the pauper's family. A drinking party is in full progress. His eyes light up at the conviviality around him, and he soon finds himself even laughing at an improper joke made by the pauper's father. But when his double's mother offers him a glass of wine, he cannot conceal his horror. Gee, he thinks, these people are wicked.

As Wally and the counterfeit Beaver do their homework in their room some days later, Eddie Haskell pays a call. "Hey, squirt," he says to the pauper, "how are things in nursery school?" At the sound of this authentic American dialect, the pauper thinks, Hey, this guy may be all right. To Eddie he says, "Listen, can you give me any tips, man? I'm working on Violet Rutherford, but I can't get past finger-banging." Eddie exchanges a questioning glance with Wally and asks, "Is that anything like going steady?" In startlement the pauper cries, "Jesus, are you guys homo?" Wally exchanges a questioning glance with Eddie and asks, "Isn't that something you do to milk?"

In the meantime, a young girl enamored of the pauper comes to his apartment looking for him. Leading Beaver into the bedroom the maiden demands, "Finger-bang me, Squirrel." "Gosh," Beaver says, "I don't want to go steady with no girl."

Let us skip a number of days until we find the mock Beaver, grown restless, at the dinner table. "Where do you go for excitement around here?" we hear him ask. Wally says, "Gosh, there's Bell Port." The pauper says, "Isn't there anyplace else around here? Heck, where is Mayfield, anyway?" Ward thoughtfully replies, "Well, the weather is always so temperate that I often suspect we might be in

California." "California?" the pauper snarls. "Hell, this isn't California. There are no junkies, no whores, no homos, no con artists, no zanies, no religious freaks, no beatniks. You can't tell me this is California, Jack."

That same night the true Beaver is discovered huddling in terror in an alley. Wearying of the gruesome fascinations of the pauper'slife, it seems that he had gone in search of familiar comforts: a bridge for spitting, a pond full of frogs, or a field for messing around. Sadly, he had had no knowledge of the vastness of the world and found himself torn between 8 bridges within the city limits, challenged by 16 ponds, and taunted by a full 32 fields. In desperation he had flown to find an old fireman for comfort and advice, but in the big city's 64 fire stations had stood 128 engines in need of polishing, tended by 256 garrulous old codgers. In the end, he could find solace only in a narrow alley where choices were impossible.

Tag: The rightful Beaver is at last restored to his true suburban domain. He discovers that he has been grounded, but after his harrowing adventures in the outside world he is content. "You know, Wally," he says, "it sure is nice to be back where every day can end in only two possible ways." Wally throws a pillow at him and knocks over the lamp, but the room remains lit.

August 13–16, 1963

In response to the Communist attack on the show, kindly Italian Pope Paul VI issued a bull calling for an international conclave to send up prayers for the aid of "that most vestal of secular entertainments, *Leave It to Beaver.*" He issued his remark in the vernacular. His bull was received with enthusiasm throughout the Free World by all but a band of right-wing Turkish terrorists.

Edith Head, the grande dame of cinematic costumers, visited Gomalco, sketchbook under arm, to design new outfits for the Cleavers. Not to take anything away from the incomparable Head, but her suggestions were ill-received. Hugh Beaumont summed it up, "Now what would we need with a lot of fancy clothes? As if Beaver needed a buccaneer costume." Miss Head left the studio in embarrassment as Ken Osmond and Frank Bank teased her ceaselessly about her last name.

That same afternoon, a delegation of Polynesian maidens visited the studio to convey Marlon Brando's fervent request to play Eddie Haskell. Ken Osmond was annoyed, saying, "You can tell your Mr. Brando that when he's lived inside Eddie Haskell's skin for six years like I have, then he can come around and try his hand at being a creep. All the Stanley Kowalskis in the world aren't creepy enough to make it in Mayfield. So until then you can tell him to get back to his motorcycles and his waterfronts." The maidens marched off to hold court with the executives.

Mosher and Connelly were holding a court of their own, with science-fiction writer Jack Finney. His plot idea for *Invasion of the Beaver Snatchers* told of an invasion of Mayfield, originally a normal American town beset by the realities of normal American towns, by outer-space pods that replace people with clean, serene, respectable duplicates devoid of personality. As Eddie Haskell remarks, "Everyone's turning into the Cleavers," who never needed to be replaced by pods. Eddie is the last holdout against the pods. When the episode ends we see him on the road between Mayfield and Bell Port screaming, "They're coming, they're coming! You're next!"

Richard Deacon insisted upon a new ending, in which a kindly but authoritative bald-headed doctor finds Eddie, believes his story, and orders Mayfield sealed off. Mosher and Connelly realized that if this story were set six years in the past, it could serve as the origin of the untroubled, anonymous, generic world of Mayfield and Bell Port. Cowriter Dick Conway suggested that a dome might have been built over the two quarantined cities to explain their lack of weather.

The idea was finally scrapped because it would have had erstwhile makeup whiz Jack Barron working himself blind trying to make everyone look six years younger. He joshed, "Just turning Jerry Mathers's oversize cranium back into the head of a cute little boy would have taken ten years off my life."

The cast was distracted from all this activity by the arrival of the next script, which appears to have been written under a pseudonym.

Beaver's Crises

Dick Checkers

Beaver finks on his friend Larry and becomes very, very popular with the class. When Miss Landers announces a class election, he is very heavily favored over Whitey Whitney for the office of class president. His one and only big mistake is agreeing to an unfair debate with Whitey in front of the class. Children being like children, they are taken in by Whitey's tousled hair, boyish grin, and normal-size head. Beaver is beaten in a very, very close election by a few very crooked ballots.

Whitey quickly leads the class down the primrose path of pink progressivism. When Beaver challenges him on the issue of free chocolate milk, Whitey pounds a PF Flyer on the desk and screams, "We will bury you!" Only Beaver's phenomenal calm in very, very tense crises enables him to get through with no more than quivering jowls.

Walking by Whitey's house on Halloween, Beaver sees him carving his pumpkin with a sickle. He hires some local derelicts to sneak into Grant Avenue Elementary School that night, steal the answers to Miss Landers's next test, and plant them in Whitey's pumpkin.

The next day at school he finks on Whitey and produces the evidence, again becoming very, very popular with his class. After Whitey is sent to reform school, Beaver receives his due: He becomes president at last.

Miss Landers keeps him after school. Being suspicious of successful people, like most intellectuals, she accuses him of having framed Whitey. "Hiring burglars is expensive," she says. "There are rumors that some rich children helped you." Beaver, having convinced himself by now that he is innocent, answers indignantly, "I want to make it perfectly clear that the only thing they ever gave me was a little dog named Nixon."

Tag: Beaver and Wally are in their bedroom playing with their new tape recorder. Wally says, "Gee, Beav, a lot of that stuff I recorded got erased." Beaver says, "Gosh Wally, I must have done it accidentally." Wally drops a pillow on him.

August 16–18, 1963

There was much speculation about Dick Checkers's real identity around Gomalco. Hugh Beaumont thought he was Barry Goldwater. Richard Deacon suggested former President Eisenhower. Barbara Billingsley argued that it must have been Ronald Reagan. "Actors can write," she said. "Look at Robert Shaw." Little marmoreal Stanley Fafara analyzed the script's style and pronounced it to be from the pen of Aldous Huxley. Jerry Mathers thought it was Sandy Koufax. The ABC executives, on the other hand, insisted they were familiar with the name and claimed Dick Checkers was one of America's foremost writers.

The issue of the new Beaver theme song was finally settled on August 18. For some weeks cocomposer Peter Rugolo had been pushing for his friends Miles Davis, Herbie Hancock, and Wayne Shorter to record a new jazzed-up Beaver theme. "Miles can bop. Bird barks when Miles bops. At the Blackhawk. Tangled with the doorman to let him in. Miles smiled."

But the original composer, Dave Kahn, objected to the new sound. He said, "I like a tune I can hum. I like to leave a situation comedy humming along to the tune. I like real music. What's wrong with a chorus of whistlers?"

Music director Stanley Wilson, when asked to decide the issue, said, "Maybe we can come up with something in between. Can this Mr. Davis whistle?"

In early August, Gomalco had received a visit from Frank Sinatra and two dark-suited associates. He brought a tape he had recorded with the Nelson Riddle Orchestra of Sammy Cahn and Jule Styne's blue-mood version of the Cleaver theme.

The autumn winds through Mayfield blow,
In Paris trees must sway,
I'll know that when I've dried her tears
I did it all my way.
My name is Ward
The young girls I once knew.
Now I'm older,
Monsieur, vermouth for two.
You know at last you're all alone
When you carry the load.
So make it one for my Beaver
And one more for the road.

Sinatra stated, "I do not think the other songs are right. They are not sad enough." Throwing his trench coat over his shoulder, he tossed a quick farewell salute and disappeared into the shadows.

Sides were quickly drawn at Gomalco. Dave Kahn and Stanley Wilson strongly favored the Sinatra version, but Pete Rugolo dissented: "Bird barked at Blue Eyes. Man can't blow. Sahara, Harrah's, *Tonight Show*. No blue eyes at the Vanguard. Dig?"

Rugolo argued for two weeks until he changed his mind on the morning of August 18, after finding his dog, Bird, legless and decapitated on his doorstep. Should the show survive, Sinatra would be in.

The latest bunch of submissions included J. D. Salinger's *Beaver in the Rye,* Irving Stone's monumental *The Agony and the Beaver,* Argentine writer Manuel Puig's *Betrayed by Jerry Mathers,* and John Fowles's *The French Beaver's Woman.* But Mosher and Connelly showed some impressive daring in slating the script by innovative Gallic sadomasochist Alain Robbe-Grillet for the next season.

Project for a Revolution in Mayfield

Alain Robbe-Grillet

Translated by S. Fafara

June and Ward are in their bedroom. June, naked, is bound to the wall by manacles. The camera moves back, and we discover that the tableau is actually a photograph in a magazine that Beaver holds in his hands. The camera then moves farther back, and we discover that this tableau is actually another photograph in another magazine that the other Cleaver boy, Wally, holds in his hands. The camera then moves slowly across the room, focusing on each item in the room at great length. So slowly does it move, in fact, that the first commercial break comes before the camera has covered more than a yard.

Ward is working in the office. Suddenly, Fred storms in, brandishing a magazine. He lays it open on Ward's desk and points out a photograph identical to the one Beaver and then Wally had held in their hands, saying, "Well, Ward old man, what have you got to say about that?" Ward does not reply. Instead, he lets his eyes rove slowly across the office. The camera follows his gaze, lingering on each object it touches upon until it arrives at the far wall where June, naked, is manacled to the wall.

Tag: Beaver, naked, is manacled to the wall of the boys'
bedroom. Methodically, Wally beats every inch of his body
with a pillow.

August 18–22, 1963

Beaumont reacted furiously to the prospect of Barbara appearing in the nude, especially considering that the boys would see her. But Barbara countered, "I think it's kind of refreshing after the way I've been desexed in the last few seasons."

For Tuesday night's entertainment on the set, pop-sociologist Alvin Toffler and chemically enlightened buffoon Timothy Leary were invited for a lecture and potluck dinner. Toffler discussed his book in progress, *Beaver Shock,* in which he enumerated the probable future repercussions of the cancellation of *Leave It to Beaver.* "Barbers will nearly go out of business in the late sixties," he prophesied.

Dr. Leary stared at the wall and giggled.

Toffler forecast, "Books and movies about political corruption will be very popular in the early seventies."

Professor Leary stared at the wall and said, "Wow."

Toffler also predicted, "Negroes will be called blacks in the near future."

Leary, a Harvard Ph.D., stared at the wall and screamed.

This dialogue was interrupted by the intrusion of television personality Charles Nelson Reilly onto the set. Reilly demanded to take Jerry Mathers's place as the Beaver. Everyone laughed derisively, but the next morning ABC executives appeared to be considering Reilly's would-be usurpation. "With the way Mathers has changed lately," they said, "perhaps Charles would bring back the cuteness that originally made Beaver popular."

The cast had had enough. They rose as a body to defend the sanctity of their television family. Connelly, Mosher, director Norman Abbot, and others came to their aid, threatening a mass strike. The executives, afraid that indispensable Richard Deacon would defect completely to *The Dick Van Dyke Show,* capitulated.

But the Screen Actors' Guild would not be mollified. It became clear that a compromise would have to be reached. From a throng of thousands of celebrated auditioners, the choices were narrowed down to two: Charles Nelson Reilly, who had endeared himself to the executives, and ageless thick-tongued vamp Mae West. By the flip of a coin, Miss West won.

Miss West was slated to play Wally's girlfriend Mary Ellen Rogers on the hoped-for seventh season. She fit in just fine. The rest of the original cast would remain together.

In the next script, Hugh Beaumont's old *confrere* Jean-Paul Sartre, paying homage to American culture, fit the American milieu of Mayfield into the style of one of his favorite authors of the past, Horace McCoy.

They Shoot Beaver, Don't They?

by Jean-Paul Sartre in the manner of
Horace McCoy

"THE STUDENT WILL ENTER," comes Mrs. Rayburn's voice. Beaver nervously enters the principal's office, holding his baseball cap in his hands. Mrs. Rayburn motions him to a chair and says, "Theodore, I'm very disappointed that you would do such a thing."

Flashback: Beaver, Larry Mondello, and Whitey Whitney share a bench in the school auditorium prior to the elementary school marathon dance. Suddenly, Larry squeals and points across the auditorium to where the girls are sitting. "Hey, look, Beaver! Judy Hensler has her legs spread and you can see her panties!" Beaver crinkles his nose in a look of disgust. "I hate icky girls." Whitey, in his high-pitched whine, says, "Well then, how come you came to the dance, Beaver? You didn't have to." Beaver says, "I came 'cause the winner gets his picture in the paper." Larry grins and says, "I know, Beaver. You came 'cause your mom made you." Beaver screams, "Did not! Did not! Did not!" Miss Landers, who will preside over the dance, glares at Beaver and he quiets down.

The music begins and Beaver and Judy are paired off. Beaver says, "I'm only dancing with you because I want to get my picture in the paper." Judy sticks out her tongue and

89

says, "Nyah! Nyah! Nyah!" They continue dancing and insulting each other viciously for the first sixteen hours, until a break is called.

The boys and girls drag off to separate rooms and collapse onto mats. They wolf down their milk and cookies. Before he dozes off, Beaver mumbles, "I hate icky girls."

The boys and girls are tiring visibly as the next session begins. The band is relentless, playing one fast polka after another. Miss Landers screams at the dancers ceaselessly, "Keep moving! Keep moving!" Suddenly, during one especially fast number, there is a commotion. Larry Mondello has collapsed. He vomits on the auditorium floor, racked with heaves. Larry is carried away, exhausted, the first casualty of the dance. The janitor arrives, pours sawdust on the vomit, and sweeps away the apple cores. The grueling dance resumes.

After the next rest period, the dancers begin dropping like flies. Beaver, in an effort to keep awake, pulls Judy's pigtails. Judy shrieks and threatens to tell.

The next day, through a haze of utter fatigue, Beaver sees his family watching him from the sidelines. Ward calls out, "Keep going, Beaver! Remember, you'll get your picture in the paper!'' June says, "Isn't it sweet to see Beaver dancing with a girl?" Wally smiles cutely and says, "I don't think he thinks it's sweet."

To add insult to injury, the following day Judy is so exhausted that Beaver has to hold her in his arms and virtually support her. Only six couples remain. Little Whitey Whitney dances by, so exhausted that his usually ashen face is nearly translucent.

The next morning marks the end of Beaver's chances. He slips on the vomit-soaked sawdust and is too exhausted to get up again. Two attendants drag Beaver and Judy outside to get some fresh air. They leave them propped up against the wall. When they finally come to, Judy whines, "Gee, Beaver. We'd have won if you weren't so stupid." Beaver rears back and punches her in the head.

Back in the principal's office, Mrs. Rayburn asks, "Why did you do such a terrible thing?" Beaver says, "Girls are icky."

Mrs. Rayburn asks, "Now what do you mean by that, Theodore?"

Beaver shrugs and says, "Gee. They shoot beaver, don't they?"

Tag: Beaver is lying on his bed recovering. Wally is combing his hair at the mirror. Beaver says, "Hey, Wally, how come they had to name that creepy thing between girls' legs after me? Why couldn't they call it an Eddie?" Wally says, "Aw, don't be such a goof, Beav," and shoots a pillow at his head.

August 22, 1963

Jeri Weil, who played Judy on the show, was greatly offended that she would have to spread her legs in front of the camera. But being firmly committed to the show, like the rest of the cast, she reluctantly agreed to do her part. Beaumont, slipping his hands thoughtfully into his pockets and rocking gently back and forth on the balls of his feet, said, "You know, it's too bad these literary scripts don't have much good wholesome entertainment in them. But that's art."

Tony Dow's patience finally ran out. Appearing before the ABC executives, he said, "Listen, we've been living on this set since the beginning of May. I'm tired of playing Monopoly and sleeping on a cot. I'm sick of Spam sandwiches. When are you going to give us the word on whether the show's really canceled or not?"

The executives promised to decide within a week. A hum of anticipation filled the lot.

Among the many submissions at this time was an idea from amusing misogynist Woody Allen. He proposed dubbing over Kurosawa's epic *Seven Samurai* with original funny dialogue read by members of the cast and a herring. The plot revolved around a band of renegades who terrorize Mayfield's denizens by attempting to convince them that a world exists around them. The Cleavers, Eddie Haskell, Lumpy Rutherford, and Larry Mondello teach them to defend their own ignorance and reassure them that beyond Bell Port and Mayfield exists only a barren wasteland.

With squeals of pride and joy, Gomalco discovered that grappa-swilling killer of animals, Ernest Hemingway, shortly before his death, had drafted a story based on the Cleavers. Although the names were different from those of the Cleaver clan, critics maintained that the likenesses were too great to be coincidental. It was a simple matter to change "Nick Adams" to "the Beaver." The author's widow submitted a treatment of the story for Gomalco's perusal.

A Clean, Well-Lighted Beaver

Ernest Hemingway

Beaver comes home from school, and June is drinking Pernod. He says, "Mom, what does *nada* mean?" June says, 'You'd better ask your father. He's in the backyard." Beaver finds Ward in safari khakis. He is cleaning his shotgun. Beaver says, "Dad, what does *nada* mean?" Ward says, "Words like *nada,* courage, and clitoris embarrass me." The shotgun goes off accidentally. The blast raises the dust from the rosebushes and then the dust settles. Beaver says, "Gee."

Beaver goes to the bedroom and Wally is practicing with his cape. His jeans are so tight they look as if he needed a shoehorn to get into them. Beaver says, "Wally, what does *nada* mean?" Wally says, "I don't know, Beav. I think it has something to do with insomnia." Beaver: "What does insomnia mean?" Wally: "That's what happens to you when you realize men die just like animals." Beaver says, "Gee," and Ward and June call the boys down to dinner.

At the table, Ward says, "This is splendid marlin." June says, "Yes, isn't it splendid?" Wally says, "Yes, it is splendid." Beaver says, "Splendid." They drink wine and Wally tells them about the fight. "It wasn't nothing much, something about homework, and then we started fighting. I slipped and Eddie had me down and choking me with both hands like he was trying to kill me and all the time I was trying to get the protractor out of my pocket to cut him loose. I got it out and I cut the muscle right across his arm and he let go of me. Then he rolled and said, 'You cut me, Sam,' and I said, '*Qué mala fortuna.*'" Beaver says, "Tuna? I thought it was marlin."

The next day Beaver visits Gus the Fireman. He asks him what *nada* means. Gus takes a sip of Pernod to cut the phlegm and in a Spanish accent says, "I like it to keep my fire station clean." Beaver says, "Huh?" and Gus says, "You have to have it, the *afición*." Beaver says, "Huh?" and Gus takes a sip of Pernod.

That night, Ward and June send the boys up to bed and sit in the living room drinking Pernod and eating olives. June suggests that they go to a cafe where they can drink Pernod and eat olives. Ward reminds her that the car isn't running. June says, "Oh, Ward. We could have had such a damn good time together." Ward says, "Yes, isn't it pretty to think so?"

Tag: The boys turn off the light and roll over, but the room remains so well lighted that Wally cannot sleep. Beaver does, and dreams about the lions.

August 23–29, 1963

More voices from the grave followed Hemingway's. From Switzerland, papers written by dreamy anima-retentive psychologist and UFO freak Carl G. Jung shortly before his death were forwarded to Gomalco by his secretary and squeeze Aniela Jaffe. Little malhued Stanley Fafara translated them from the original German. In *Cleavers of Transformation,* Jung intoned, "It is through Beaver as the amphibious mammal, half in the seas of unconsciousness and half pushed bucktoothed into the angular circumscription of ego-consciousness that June transforms the quaternion. In her enantiodromia the Cleavers transcend into the mandala and all Mayfield is integrated into the porcine completeness of Larry Mondello."

Shortly after, Doris Packer, who played Mrs. Rayburn, the principal of Grant Avenue Elementary School, claimed to have been visited by the disembodied head and knees of popular necromancer Edgar Cayce. In a voice that Packer described as sounding "like a foghorn on a clear night," Cayce cautioned, "Let not the Beaver touch haddock to his lips ere a fortnight has lapsed." Mathers, who never ate whiting in deference to little color-starved Stanley Fafara, alternated between turbot and fillet of sole for the next two weeks. Sand dabs were unavailable.

A week after their talk with Tony Dow, the ABC executives again put off their decision on cancellation to go to a fish fry up at the lake. The cast began to feel like

Tantalus with the prospect of continuation always just beyond their grasp. But the spirits of those camping on the set were buoyed by the boundless enthusiasm of the world's literary and cinematic community. They received Jerzy Kosinski's script *The Painted Beaver,* Isaac Bashevis Singer's *Beaver the Fool,* Neil Simon's *The Odd Family,* and Jacqueline Susann's *Valley of the Beavers.*

The standout, however, was filmmaker Michael Cacoyannis's drama of passion and feta cheese in the spirit of the greatest of Greek novelists.

Beaver the Greek

by Michael Cacoyannis in the manner of
Nikos Kazantzakis

At the breakfast table, Wally tells Ward and June of his new job, building a cookhouse at Friend's Lake with Eddie Haskell. June says, "Isn't that an awfully big job for boys your age?" Wally says, "Shucks, Mom, we're big enough to handle it. Besides, I'm tired of being a passive theologian." He finishes his lamb and olives and rushes off, eager for a physical rite of passage.

At the lake, Wally does what he is told unquestioningly, but Eddie spends half his time at the shore, drinking retsina and eating olives. The supervisor, in black boots, black cap, and black moustache, tells him he should go home until he grows up. Someone on the lakeshore plays a bongo-party record and Eddie dances wildly until he collapses.

That night, on the shore, Eddie and Wally eat feta cheese and olives, and Eddie speaks. "The people, they say, 'That Eddie Haskell, he is a madman. When he wants to join the merchant marine and he chickens out, he dances. When he wants his own apartment and his old man and his landlady and all his friends talk him into going home, he dances. When he calls a girl for a date and she tells him she has to go to the dentist on Friday night, then he is like a madman, and he dances.' But if I did not dance I would die.

They say a boy should tire of being a creep and should sit quietly and ask Respectability to lead him away. But when Respectability comes to me I will fight it and I, Eddie Haskell, I will tear the letters off its very sweater."

In a rage, Eddie leaps up and wrestles a goat.

Beaver runs by, crying, "Hey, Wally! Me and a bunch of the guys are gonna go throw rocks at Mary Ellen Rogers! You wanna come?"

Wally follows in morbid fascination. He watches helplessly as Beaver and his little friends stone his girl friend. When Beaver decapitates her, Wally says, "Gee, Beav, you're really going to get it now."

The next morning Eddie is on the shore, drinking raki and eating olives. Wally comes to join him, stricken with grief. Shyly, he says, "Eddie, teach me to dance." Spreading their arms until their hands touch, they dance by the water to the *Beaver* theme song.

Tag: Beaver is eating unleavened bread and olives on the bed. Wally is practicing his bouzouki at the desk. Beaver says, "You know, Wally, that Eddie Haskell isn't such a creepy guy after all." Wally says, "How's that, Beav?" Beaver says, "Well, the way I figure is, if you've gotta dance, at least Eddie's way you don't have to dance with girls." Wally laughs and hits him with a goat.

August 29–September 1, 1963

Concerning *Valley of the Beavers,* Mosher fretted, "Me and Joe, we sure didn't like seeing the kids popping all those pills. Method acting is fine, but, whoa, they took it too far if you ask us."

"Hey, if we film *The Painted Beaver,*" queried Rusty Stevens, "do I get to eat the beaver carcass?" Batman's Aunt Harriet, who played Larry's mother, cautioned, "Now, Rusty, you make sure you skin that beaver so the paint won't poison you."

More and more parties were showing an interest in the *Beaver* project. Federico Fellini, impresario of Italian freak shows, sought to woo Frank Bank away for his new movie, *La Dolce Vita,* to play opposite Anita Ekberg. Marcello Mastroianni, of whom Fellini had grown tired, was all too happy to switch places with Bank in playing Lumpy Rutherford, going so far as to offer to gain 209 pounds for the role. Richard Deacon vetoed the entire plan. Fellini sailed back to Italy despondent.

Playboy magazine offered $1.6 million each to Barbara Billingsley and Sue "Miss Landers" Randall to adorn their centerfolds in successive months, Barbara dressed only in pearls and high heels, Sue nude and covered with chalk dust. Billingsley declined at Hugh Beaumont's good-natured insistence. Randall felt too embarrassed at showing her toes in a national magazine.

Critic Lionel Endenberry, LittD., of the *Perth Review,* donated an article entitled "Beaver: Child, Rodent, or Organ?" Unfortunately, his work is inconclusive; it only explains how Beaver can be none of the three. Pointing out that the human personality is established by the age of four, he immediately ruled out Beaver, who had reached thirteen with no luck, from the status of child. He noted that Beaver "possesses the requisite buckteeth of the rodent, but lacks the flat tail and webbed toes of his rodent namesake." Lastly, he observed that Beaver shared with the organ of that name his messy hair and pink lips, but that "the hair is not kinky enough nor are the lips elastic enough to squeeze a baby out."

Murder buff James M. Cain contributed the first script of the new month.

The Beaver Always Rings Twice

James M. Cain

Ward and Miss Landers are making violent love on Mrs. Rayburn's desk. When they finish, they sing an aria in C major, Ward taking the falsetto and Miss Landers the tenor. When the song is over they are seized by a desire to kill June. They plot to bury her alive in Metzger's Field. That excites them, and they make love again. She bleeds. The next day Ward gets everything ready but at the last minute misplaces the shovel and the crime has to be postponed.

The following morning June glances out the window at a motorcycle policeman who is racing by on the street. She happens to glance down and spots the shovel hidden in the rosebushes. She realizes everything and is overwhelmed with lust for Fred Rutherford. She invites him over and they make vicious love on Wally's desk. Afterward they sing an aria from *La Boheme* and plot to drown Ward in Miller's Pond. They make love again, and Fred bleeds. No mail arrives that day.

Fred gets everything in readiness the next day but misplaces his swimming trunks. At the office, Ward glances out the window at a cat who has just meowed and spots the swimming trunks hidden behind the trash can. He realizes everything and decides, in addition to June, to kill Fred, Lumpy, Whitey Whitney, and Gus the Fireman. Meanwhile,

Beaver has decided to kill Miss Landers and Gilbert; Richard has resolved to kill Eddie Haskell and June; and Wally is hell-bent on doing in Mary Ellen Rogers, Mrs. Rayburn, and the Beaver.

The next day they all arrive at Metzger's Field, armed to the teeth. Ward strikes the first blow, bringing a sap down on Fred's bald pate. Fred is unharmed. Everybody laughs and agrees to forget the whole thing. A cat appears and rubs itself against Whitey Whitney's legs. They all join in on an operatta.

Tag: Wally, studying at his desk, does not notice Beaver slipping a blackjack into a pillowcase. Thinking that the pillowcase contains only a pillow, he makes no attempt to duck when Beaver swings it at his head. Beaver coldcocks him.

September 2–5, 1963

The purveyors of America's pop culture converged on Gomalco in the waning days of summer. Stan Lee, the grinning figurehead of American comic books, announced that Marvel Comics hoped to launch *The Amazing Beaver-Man*. Bitten by a radioactive beaver, meek Theodore Cleaver acquires all the powers of a human rodent and fights such colorfully costumed villains as Captain Soup Bowl, Doctor Toes, Fire-Man, and The Creep, who, in a melodramatic twist, is really the best friend of his brother Wally. Most of those involved, being longtime readers of the Superman line of comics, denounced the idea as tasteless. Dissenting was diminutive pasty Stanley Fafara, who argued for the validity of Marvel Comics as an art form and snapped, "The Marvel line of magazines should not even be compared with some Nietzschean aberration prancing about in a red and blue jumpsuit." Good-natured arguments went on for several days.

Little doughy Stanley Fafara's big myopic brother Tiger Fafara, who played Wally's friend Tooey in the early seasons, defied his hypercerebral brother in bringing the next guests: William Hanna and Joseph Barbera, popular degraders of the art of animation. They requested the rights to produce a Saturday-morning cartoon show featuring the Cleaver clan and a snickering dog.

Most notably, Walt Disney, lover of mice and sundry rodents, sauntered into the Gomalco offices bearing tidings of a grandiose plan: a Beaverland amusement park to be located in the Ozark Mountains near Little Rock, Arkansas. Sprawling over 1,370 acres, it wouldappear at first glance to be a massive suburban housing tract. But closer examination would reveal a myriad of delightful rides and amusements in the finest Disney tradition, divided into many theme parks: Metzger's Field, Fire Stationland, Haskell Country, Grant Avenue Elementaryland, and quaint old Mayfield Square. Featured among the rides would be a Soup Bowl Coaster, a Carousel of Creeps, and an Autorama highlighting miniature duplicates of Lumpy's jalopy. Merry visitors would be welcomed by teenage actors wearing huge papier-mâché heads fashioned in the likenesses of the cast, including an exceptionally humongous bucktoothed mask of Theodore Cleaver. Stuffed beavers galore would be awarded to lucky winners at such games of skill as the Pillow Toss, Spit-off-the-Bridge, and Getting Out of Trouble.

At the park's very center would stand a monumental version of the Cleaver home, including a cavernous den through which gleeful guests would stroll and hear tape-recorded lectures by Ward. Uncle Walt, imagining the completed masterwork, said wistfully, "Nothing warms my heart like the innocent mirth of laugh tracks."

The park's tour de force was to be a series of Audio-Animatronic robots of the Cleaver clan of the type Disney would later introduce to his less spectacular Disneyland and Walt Disney World. Plans were drawn up, but after careful study it was decided that the robots were unrealistic. Although they were unable to speak or move, they nevertheless displayed more vitality and character than the show's regulars were ever known to possess.

That very same afternoon, Bertrand Russell sent in his new book, *Why I Am Not a Cleaver,* but in the excitement no one read it.

One muggy afternoon, they opened the mail to find a sultry drama of atrophied lives and arson in decaying Mayfield by the histrionic Southern playwright, Tennessee Williams.

Beaver on a Hot Tin Roof

Tennessee Williams

A school bus pulls up in front of the Cleaver residence. June is standing on the porch, barefoot and in her slip. Beaver leaves the bus, saying, "Mama, Miss Landers is coming over for some beers later on." June swats at a fly.

In the boys' bedroom, Wally, Big Ward, Eddie, Lumpy, and Mary Ellen Rogers are playing strip poker and eating off a cold plate. Mary Ellen Rogers is down to her petticoat. A flamingo is embroidered over her left breast. Beaver throws his books on the bed and says, "Miss Landers is coming over later on for some beers." Big Ward says, "I'll hump her from hell to breakfast," and swats at a fly.

That evening, a school bus pulls up in front of the Cleaver residence. June is standing on the porch, barefoot and in her slip. Miss Landers leaves the bus, fanning herself, and says, "A delicate flower like me simply wilts in this heat." She doesn't notice Larry, Whitey, Gilbert, Richard, and Beaver hiding in the old family tree. There is a tarantula embroidered over her left breast.

Larry says, "Gosh, look! She's got toes!" and swats at an iguana.

Whitey says, "Look how that red paint glows against her lily-white toes."

Beaver says, "I could take that paint off her toes and make her like it."

As the cold dinner with Big Ward and June progresses, Miss Landers gazes into space and talks of graveyards and yellowing love letters. She says, "I have always depended upon the kindness of Cleavers." Everyone ignores her. Halfway through dinner they all pause to watch the house next door burn down. Big Ward idly fondles Miss Landers's lily-white buttocks. Miss Landers says, "Oh, look how the flames dance, like colored lights." Big Ward says, "That's what Polacks see when they hump." June adjusts the strap of her slip, swats at a fly, and says, "Don't be crude." Big Ward says, "I have a Polack acquaintance who can testify to that."

Miss Landers runs from the house in tears. The boys drop from the tree, kill her with stones, and devour her.

Tag: Wally is sitting at his desk sweating. Beaver, sweating, sneaks up behind him and fires a cap gun by his ear. Wally hits him with a soggy yellow lace pillow, and we hear carousel music.

September 5–7, 1963

Sue Randall was titillated at the prospect of being devoured. Rusty Stevens, gulping down a melon, was ecstatic after the meaning of devoured was explained to him. "Gee, do we really get to eat Sue? Do we?"

Mathers, looking rather confused, asked, "Isn't Tennessee Williams a cartoon penguin?"

It was on the balmy afternoon of September 7 that what later proved to be the last script of the Summer of the Beaver arrived. If the great phase of American literature can be said to have begun with Sherwood Anderson, then it is only fitting that this script by Ray Bradbury, the Sherwood Anderson of space, should mark its end.

The Mayfield Chronicles

Ray Bradbury

The first expedition. A plane lands in Metzger's Field. Beaver runs home to tell the family. They all exchange alarmed glances. June, tentatively, says, "Why, I suppose it could have come from Bell Port." Wally says, "Gee, Mom, you could just ride your bike from Bell Port." Ward says, "But ... where else is there?"

June is in the living room talking on the phone. She says, "Why, yes, Mrs. Mondello ... I'm very curious, too. Ward thinks they come from beyond ... He thinks they may be very different there ... Certainly, they may even know of different activities. Come to think of it, I do get awfully tired of lining shelves and stirring pots..." Ward, overhearing, grimly takes a five iron from the closet and leaves the house.

He returns that night just as the family is about to start dinner. His five iron is blood-smeared. Taking his place at the head of the table, he says, "Fred Rutherford and I did something we didn't want to do. But it comes with being a husband and a father." June looks crestfallen and serves the peas. Ward says, "June, you must understand. When we came upon them they were drinking beer, spanking their children, and discussing politics. What else could we do, dear?"

The second expedition. A plane lands secretly at Friend's Lake. Two men disembark. One is smoking a cigarette, the other is drinking a cocktail from a can. One says, "So that's it down there, huh?" The other says, "I wonder what the hell could have happened to the first expedition. Not one damn word since the first transmission." Just then, the sound of bongos comes from the shore. Following the sound, they find a curly-haired young man. The first man, relieved, says, "He looks real enough. He might be a survivor."

Cautiously, they emerge from the thicket. The young man stops playing and says, "Hey, Gertrude. Are you hep to the beat?" One man asks, "Are you from around here?" The young man looks at them mystified. Then he says, "Okay, I get it, Sam. You mean, am I from Mayfield or Bell Port, right?" The men eye each other suspiciously. The first asks, "You mean everyone around here is from Mayfield or Bell Port? There's nobody here from, say ... New York? Philadelphia? Los Angeles?" The young man looks momentarily perplexed and then says, "Sure, Alvin, sure. New Angeles. I've heard of that. My old man gives me the bread to go there all the time." The man asks, "But do you know anyone who's come from there?" The young man says, "Right this way, cats."

He leads them to the golf course at the end of the lake. The first man says to the other, "He seems all right, not like the other natives we've heard described. No letterman sweater, no cute smile, no chaperon." The other says, "Yeah, but there's something wrong. He still isn't quite three-dimensional. Let's test him." He calls to the young man, "Sure is a damned hot day, isn't it?" The young man looks at them, confused. "Sure is a what hot day?" As the men back away in horrified realization, Ward and Fred rise behind them and club them down with five irons.

The third expedition. Four men slip into the streets of Mayfield in the rosy morning. They are all disguised in ties and golf sweaters. They hear the tinkle of lemonade being stirred behind screen doors. They see a pug-nosed boy in a letterman sweater pushing a lawn mower. A man in a tie and golf sweater comes out grinning to get the paper. One man whispers, "I think it's a trap. A two-dimensional imitation of our sappiest fantasies about a small American town." Another points and says, "But look at them now."

The others turn and see a housewife in a dress and high heels smile over her shoulder and carry a picnic basket to a station wagon. The man in the golf sweater follows her with a Thermos, smiles back at the door, and takes the driver's seat. The pug-nosed boy, towel in hand, leaps a hedge with a smile, looks over his shoulder, and gets in the back seat. Last of all, a cute little boy with a big head dashes for the car and jumps in the back. As the car backs from the driveway, the boy turns and smiles through the rear window, showing two enormous buckteeth.

"My God," says one of the men. "I think it's real." They all flee in horror.

Tag: In their bedroom, the boys hear the droning of an engine. They dash to the window to see the plane taking off from the woods. Wally turns off the light and the room remains bright, although the night sky is empty of moon, stars, and planets.

Epilogue

In the last twenty years, television has been graced by a number of worthwhile programs. Critics have acclaimed such shows as *The Smothers Brothers, All in the Family, The Waltons, M*A*S*H,* and *Hill Street Blues.* But none of these, despite the excellence they attained within their limits, transcended those very limits. None of them transformed television into a medium to be reckoned with. None of them fired the enthusiasm of the world's literati the way *Leave It to Beaver* would have, had it been allowed to live.

Surely, had the scripts in this book been utilized in a seventh *Beaver* season, they would have sparked a marriage of literature and television. What writer, having witnessed the artistic heights attained by *Leave It to Beaver,* could have failed to see the vast potential inherent in other weekly television series? Seeing a new opportunity to bring his themes before the general public, how could Jerzy Kosinski have passed up the opportunity to write for *Bewitched?* Surely James Baldwin would have been elated to write scripts for *The Jeffersons.* Joyce Carol Oates, evincing her fascination for the psychology of family life, would have leaped at the chance to pen scripts for *The Brady Bunch.* Jean-Paul Sartre, that master of existential merriment, would have been a natural for the No Exit situation of *Gilligan's Island.* And what sensible viewer would have changed the channel after seeing an episode of *Me and the Chimp* credited to Nobel Prize-winner Saul Bellow?

But such literary pyrotechnics were not destined to be. On September 8, 1963, the ABC executives stuck their heads into the Gomalco lot and announced, "You can all pack up and go home now. *Leave It to Beaver* has been canceled." With those words, an era came to an end. A hush fell over the lot. Then the cast began to weep. And the world wept with them.

The world may have wept, but you don't have to!
Here's a sneak peek at the long-awaited sequel,
The Beaver Papers 2…

September 8, 1963

The sounds of weeping filled the air over Gomalco. Hugh Beaumont, who played Ward Cleaver on the show, looked over the lot that had been the site of so many hopes throughout the summer and turned his face away from the others so that they could not see his tears. Jerry Mathers, the Beaver himself, tried to take it like a man, but as soon as his eyes met the tear-filled gaze of Barbara Billingsley, the actress who had immortalized the role of his mother, June Cleaver, he too broke down.

As afternoon turned to dusk, the sounds of grief gave way to a mournful silence. All the residents of that once-boisterous camp turned to taking down their tents, rolling up their sleeping bags, and packing up their cooking and sporting equipment. But then one voice shattered the silence. "Are we gonna let this beat us?" it exhorted. "Are we gonna let everything that Beaver means to the world die just because a few old guys in suits tell us to get lost?"

The voice belonged to Tony Dow, who played Wally, the Cleavers' confident and athletic older son. He had leaped atop one of the ping pong tables and posed there glaring challengingly at the assembled group. Shaking his fist, he said, "So what if ABC canceled us? There's still CBS and NBC!" When Jerry Mathers pointed out that ABC had only begun broadcasting the show after CBS had canceled it five years before, Tony shook his fist again and said, "So there's still NBC, isn't there?"

Hugh Beaumont had been looking on worriedly. "Now Tony," he called, "there's no sense in getting yourself worked up." But for once, Tony would not listen to his surrogate father. Leaping off the table, he strode to the stack of scripts that had been pouring in since May and started searching through them frantically. "I'm going to take the best script we've got straight to NBC—and when they see it, you can bet they'll see what those lunkheads at ABC can't!" Soon enough he found the script he considered the best of all, which happened to be one that focused almost entirely on Wally. Written by James Leo Herlihy, it told a powerful tale of friendship, coconuts, and closeted homoeroticism.

Midnight Beaver

James Leo Herlihy

In the cowboy boots that Aunt Martha sent him for Christmas, Wally Cleaver is nearly five foot ten and life is different. For a year he's been wrestling with what he thought would be the biggest decision of his life, whether to go to State or Valley, but looking at himself in the mirror he knows that State and Valley combined don't have room in them for a Wally Cleaver.

Lumpy Rutherford has told him that men in the city are just faggots mostly, and so the rich city women have to pay for what they want. Wally is unclear on what a faggot is, but he's fairly sure he isn't one, especially in his tall boots, Stetson hat, western shirt, and fringed letterman sweater, and so the city women will pay plenty if he gives them what they want.

The man at the bus station just looks at him blankly when he says, "I want a ticket to the city." Wally is unsure of what cities Mayfield might be near, and so he tells the man the name of the one place he knows of for sure, which is Bell Port, and an hour later he's striding through the streets of the town wondering if Bell Port is big enough to hold a Wally Cleaver. He's a beautiful animal, this Wally Cleaver, with his pug nose and curly hair and what all the

Mayfield High girls call dreamy eyes. But he's not hunting for high school girls now.

"Beg pardon, ma'am," he drawls to a very fat woman with a very small poodle. "I'm new in town and looking for a lady who'll pay for what she wants." The woman laughs in his face, and Wally blushes crimson.

At a soda fountain he knocks back shots of chocolate malted, chasing them down with root beer. Then he hears an annoying voice at his elbow. "Where'd you get that shirt, Elwood? Your Aunt Martha?"

"Eddie!" Wally says. "What in heck are you doing in Bell Port?" Eddie tells him how he got tired of the small time in Mayfield and headed where an operator could make some real money. "O' course, this dump's just a stepping stone. I'm heading for Florida, where a man can live on coconuts and sunshine and not break his ass for nothin'." Wally isn't clear where Florida is, but he asks, "And have they got women there who'll pay plenty for what they want?" Eddie looks at Wally with a new respect. "Say, Loverboy, you're not as square as you look. You're a hustler!" "Hey, I may dress like a cowboy," Wally says indignantly, "but I never stole a head of cattle in my life!"

Just then they're interrupted by two young men with plucked eyebrows and menacing stares. "Didn't expect to see you come back here, Creepo." "My name is not Creepo!" Eddie screams. "My name is Edward Clark Haskell!" But he hurries away, and as Wally follows he notices that Eddie is limping badly and launching into a sickening wet cough. "Geez, Eddie," he says, "since when are you a tubercular cripple?" "I'm not a cripple, I'm a gimp! And this cough's nothin' a trip to Florida won't fix!"

He leads Wally into the condemned building where he's been holing up. Night falls and the cruel cold stabs through Wally like no cold he's ever felt. With a pang of longing he remembers Mayfield and its lack of weather. Eddie, downing cough syrup like it was liquor, shares his street smarts. "These rich suburban chicks can't be cruisin' Bell Port Square looking at the merchandise if they want to be able to show their faces at the next PTA meeting. You follow me, Einstein? You need a middleman, an agent, a representative."

"Gee, I don't know, Eddie," Wally says. "This sounds like one of those nutty schemes of yours that get me in trouble. Like that time Dad tried to teach me about the stock market and you talked me into investing in that rocket factory." Eddie snorts derisively and starts telling him how he can spot a woman who wants a cowboy in her bed. Wally snorts in laughter. "In her *bed*? Why in heck would she want me there?"

Eddie yells, "You got a tin ass, Cornelius? What do you *think* you'll be doing when chicks pay you for what they want?" Wally shrugs. "Shucks, I don't know. All those things women want. Mowing their lawns, washing their cars, taking out their trash."

Eddie goes into a hideous coughing fit. His teeth chatter and he sweats a river. Wally wraps him in his own fringed sweater and heats cough syrup over Sterno, but it's clear that Eddie can't last much longer. He croaks one word. "Florida."

Knowing he has no choice, Wally takes to the midnight streets, standing on one corner after another until an effeminate older man catches his eye. "Evening, son. Has anyone ever told you that you have dreamy eyes?" Wally says, "I need money, mister. I'll do anything to get it. Anything."

An hour later Wally has finished scraping down the man's backyard grill and the man has given him ten dollars and a St. Christopher medal. He drags Eddie to the station and onto a bus. After a while, Eddie pees in his pants and says, "Sorry, Clyde, but I'm never gonna make it all the way to Florida." "That's okay," Wally says. "The bus driver doesn't know where Florida is anyway." Before Eddie can answer, they pull into the warmth of the Mayfield station.

Tag: Wally is filling out his application to State when he notices Beaver preening in the mirror. In the cowboy boots that Aunt Martha sent him for Christmas, he's nearly five foot four and thinks life is different. "Cut it out, Beav. You'll never make it as a male hustler." "Oh yeah?" Beaver sneers. "Now that Creepo's leg is all better, he says he's gonna set me up with every pansy in Florida!" "Aw, come off it!" Wally laughs. "What do you know about gardening?" he throws a pillow that knocks Beaver's Stetson clean off his head.

September 8-9, 1963

The Herlihy script in hand, Tony ran to the nearby pile of rejected props, pulled out the fringed letterman sweater that had been crafted for that very episode in the hopeful days of early summer, and made for the door. Hugh Beaumont tried to intercept him, but the youngster eluded him, thanks to all the track and field practice that he engaged in as part of his rigorous training to bring verisimilitude to Wally Cleaver.

Hugh told the group, "I'm afraid Tony's only setting himself up for more disappointment. I wish I'd been able to have a man-to-man talk with him about accepting reality. I wouldn't feel right about leaving until I know he's back safely, so I'll wait. But the rest of you can go on packing if you want." Most of the others went back to their melancholy work, but then Barbara Billingsley announced that if she left she'd only be worrying about Tony, too. Ken Osmond, who played Wally's best friend Eddie Haskell, echoed her sentiments. By nightfall, only a few crew members had left the encampment.

As it turned out, the impulsive Tony had decided to camp at NBC's Burbank studio until he got an audience with the executives, and by the next morning he had not returned. Everyone awoke to discover not only his absence, but that the morning papers all carried the news that *Leave It to Beaver* was no more. "I had woken up in my tent half-believing it was all a terrible dream," said Madge Blake, who portrayed the mother of Beaver's best friend Larry. "When I saw it right there in the headlines, I started crying all over again."

Then the mail delivery brought its usual spate of submissions from the literary and artistic worlds, and for a brief shining moment many others wondered if it had all been a bad dream, too. But when Burt Mustin, the character actor who gave life to old Gus the Fireman, pointed out that they all must have been mailed before word of the series's cancellation had broken, grim reality returned. Among the scripts were Carson McCullers's *The Beaver Is a Lonely Hunter*, Ralph Ellison's *Invisible Beaver*, and Richard Brautigan's *Trout Fishing in Mayfield*. Most of the gang felt too heavy-hearted even to glance at them, but Jerry Mathers, to take his mind off the agonizing wait, opened a package that contained a script from fledgling New Journalist Tom Wolfe.

The Electric Kool-Aid Kleaver Picnic
Tom Wolfe

So the door to this impossibly 100 percent perfect Middle
Class house opens and out glides this cool chick in chiffon
and pearls, a picnic basket rocking so daintily and
weightlessly over her arm that you'd never think it could
contain enough food to feed a sparrow, let alone a family of
four. She looks over her shoulder and here comes a cat that
you can tell right off is as mad as a hatter, wearing this hip
golf-sweater-and-slacks ensemble and the...shoes—how
they shine!—and cradling a pint-sized cooler. He does the
same twist-and-gape and out bounds this teenager in
checked shirt and these crazy white chinos that proclaim
MOD FREAK as if written in Day-Glo letters, toting a
towel and looking extraordinarily like Bucky Barnes, if you
remember him from the comics. He looks over his shoulder
too, and out flies the coolest, gawkiest, biggest-headed kid
you ever saw, leaping a hedge, diving into that Bauhaus-
sleek Plymouth Fury, and then, as it backs right at you,
beaming through the back window like a buck-toothed
Cheshire Cat on the dread LSD!

Beautiful...the current fantasy...the Merry Kleavers out
for a picnic!

The Plymouth blazing through a Mondrian painting of
white sidewalks and green lawns (Huxley's reducing valve

irrigating the suburban dream!), everywhere crazy-grinning dads zipping around with clippers, Apollonian lads pushing lawn mowers. And here come the moms, in cocktail dresses and high heels, bearing trays laden with these beaded pitchers full of what you know must be Kool-Aid. And now the Kleavers hit the shopping district. The Mayfield Bank! The Mayfield Drug Store! The Mayfield Church! And here's the Mayfield Malt Shoppe with its gleaming Formica counter, serving pure vanilla teens. Business cats walking down the street in matching suits and a slick mom pushing a streamlined baby in a tangerine-flake stroller. Man, it's so perfectly American Small Town that it just has to be a put-on! And look, there's the Mayfield Bookstore. For a minute you expect to see Kerouac's *On the Road* and the *Tibetan Book of the Dead* and I Ching yarrow stalks displayed in the window…but you don't! And that's just it…you don't! It's all so studiedly unhip that it's the hippest place on earth!

Haul ass, and there they are, past the Mayfield city limits. But where is this Mayfield? California? Ohio? Nobody knows. You look for clues: there's Friend's Lake, Camelback Cutoff, Crystal Falls, Bell Port. And that's it. You know it's not the South, because the skin tones here are as monochrome as a Barnett Newman painting (and they still talk about that wedding reception where they first heard of the Langleys' Negro maid). But do they care where they are? Why would they?!

Ward, the holy primitive, the *natural*, sits hunched over the wheel in a kind of kinetic trance. June, the eternal beatific pioneer wife, pats his arm and turns in her seat to smile that Mother Earth smile at the boys. And the boys…the BOYS! How to tell it…the current fantasy? Anticipation? Hell no!

It's a NOW TRIP. It's a risk-all balls-out plunge into the country, whether it appears on any map or not. That's the way it is in the careening, crazy-dreaming rhythm of the car, everything becoming allegorical, understood only deep in the KLEAVER MIND. And the meaning is this: You're either on the picnic...or you're off the picnic.

The leaves are changing color, a cataclysmic clash of seasons, Dr. Strange vs. Baron Mordo! Anyway, that's the way the kid describes it, the cool kid with the big head, and the others get it right away. That's the way it is with the Merry Kleavers. They pick up on the most banal comments as if they were metaphors for life, all their lives becoming more fabulous every minute like the most fabulous TV show. It's phony, goddamn it...but...after a while it just gets to you, like if their lives were syndicated you'd make time every day out of your own life to tune in on the fruits of love and euphoria and cornball humor.

The cool kid with the big head says, "Hey, Dad. Are we almost there?"

And the dad says, "Just a little further, Beav."

Further! But exactly! It's what Joachim Wach called "the experience of the holy." What George Webber called the "possession of the deity." What Eddie Haskell, with that zoned-out stoned-out madcap simplicity, would term "crazy, Lionel!" But better to back off. To define it is to limit it. FURTHER.

That's all. Period.

Tag: Beaver peels back the covers from his bed and says, "Gee, Wally. Until our picnic today I never realized what a hip family we are." Wally says, "Heck yeah we're hip,

Beav. Do you think a hip young representative of the New Journalism with a Ph.D. from Yale and a wild Edwardian jacket would hang out with us all day if we weren't?" Wally flips off the light, but the room remains crazily lit, as if Salvador Dali, spinning like a dervish, had daubed the air itself with mad streaks of Day-Glo paint.

Continued in

The Beaver Papers 2

The Fall of the Beaver

On sale now from Atomic Drop Press!

Million Dollar Ideas

Will Jacobs & Gerard Jones

It's post-World War II Hollywood, and Ed and Johnny have proven themselves the fastest rewrite-men in town— except that they're not content to be doctoring the scripts of other writers and are burning to sell original screenplays in which they can showcase their inventive genius. But there's a catch. Their ideas aren't simply inventive, they're downright outlandish—not to mention oddly anachronistic. Who ever heard of making a movie about homosexual cowboys in 1946? Certainly not the moguls who run the big studios. Before they know it, Ed and Johnny have become pariahs.

But will they give up their dreams? Not when a relic from Hollywood's silent era is looking to make a comeback and can't find a single respectable screenwriter who'll give him the time of day. So a partnership is born—one that throws the past and future together in an unforgettable brew.

With appearances by Howard Hughes, Betty Grable, Preston Sturges, Raymond Chandler, Tor Johnson, Philip K. Dick, Bertolt Brecht, and a cast of thousands.

The Mystery of the Changin' Times
Will Jacobs & Gerard Jones

All readers from 16 to 96 who like lively stories, packed with humor and satire, will want to read the latest book by Jacobs and Jones. Featuring the Sturdy Boys, sons of a famous American detective, it reveals what happens when the times start a-changin' in the 1960s and Balmy Bay, the boys' idyllic home, is suddenly invaded by the denizens of a weird new "counterculture."

In seven complete mysteries, all building to a single, startling climax, you will see America's brightest boy detectives try to expose the smuggling operation that they know must lie behind the claims of the weird "Black Panthers" to be "empowering their race"...uncover the foreign mind-control techniques that must be driving a college professor to turn his students against America's heroic efforts to end Communism in Vietnam...and the nefarious scheme that lies behind the sudden desire of young women to discard their foundation garments—and with them fulfilling lives of housewifery.

The Sturdy Boys have helped solve many thrilling cases after school hours and during vacations, but will they stand a chance against the agents of social change?

My Pal Splendid Man

Will Jacobs & Gerard Jones

Will Jones is an aspiring writer with a love of literature who doesn't get out much. Splendid Man is the most powerful being in the universe who has very little time for himself. But when they become pals, Will tutors Splendid Man in the fine arts while Splendid Man helps Will meet girls, introduces him to his costumed colleagues, and takes him on jaunts through space and time.

See what happens when Splendid Man whisks Will off to visit the ancient library of Alexandria…when Will talks Splendid Man out of a profound funk after they see a movie version of his life that portrays him as a dark, modern hero…and when the most powerful teenage girl in the universe develops a crush on our bookish protagonist. Through it all, Splendid Man harbors a deep secret—will his new pal ever learn the truth?

In fifteen interconnected short stories, with humor both affectionate and absurd, Jacobs and Jones portray a collision of the very fantastic and the very ordinary as only they can.

My Tongue Is Quick

Will Jacobs & Gerard Jones

What happens when a two-fisted private eye wades into the brutal jungle of the poetry business? Why do the world's greatest novelists suddenly start writing better fiction when the author of a boys' detective series goes missing? Such are the questions Will Jacobs and Gerard Jones tackle in stories originally published in the *National Lampoon* and collected here for the first time.

Also included are three new adventures of the improbable costars of *My Pal Splendid Man*: Will Jones, an aspiring writer who doesn't get out much, and Splendid Man, the most powerful being in the universe, who helps his pal develop a social life as his pal tutors him about literature.

Finally, Ed and Johnny, heroes of *Million Dollar Ideas*, those indefatigably hustling screenwriters determined to set postwar Hollywood on fire with their highly original—and oddly anachronistic—movie ideas, return for six new stories. Their latest schemes bring them into collision with American icons ranging from William Faulkner to Stepin Fetchit to the Red-baiting agents of the FBI.

The Max Kleinman Reader

Will Jacobs, Gerard Jones & James W. Zook

Max Kleinman is a skid-row genius who from 1946 to 1999 produced 30,000 poems, most of them wrapped around his singular obsessions with fallen nuns, shrapnel wounds, Western philosophy, cheap wine, and All-Star Wrestling.

But does Max Kleinman really exist? Or is he only the twisted invention of maverick scholar Lionel Endenberry? Endenberry claims to have found a shoebox containing all these documents in a garage sale in Van Nuys, California. He exults at having "discovered a soon-to-be notable literary figure," and calls Kleinman a poet of "enormous versatility and vigor." But after months of searching for further evidence of the shadowy genius's existence, he claims to have found not a trace.

The Max Kleinman Reader features the best of those 30,000 poems, along with a cryptic autobiography, a bizarre interview, and a handful of unsettling photographs. But whether any of these answer the questions about Kleinman's existence is a matter best left up to the reader.

www.ingramcontent.com/pod-product-compliance
Lightning Source LLC
Chambersburg PA
CBHW051249170626
46809CB00004B/1568